This Was Nevada

This Was NEVADA

Phillip I. Earl

Introduction by
PETER L. BANDURRAGA

RENO: NEVADA HISTORICAL SOCIETY: 1986

*To my wife Jean, my son Kevin, and my
daughter Kira, who share my love of
Nevada and have had a full part in
everything that has gone into this project.*

Contents

Acknowledgements

THE PUBLICATION of this book was facilitated by a grant from Rollan and Marilyn Melton of Reno. A decent respect for the history of history compels me to chronicle the manner in which this came about. Two years ago, one of Rollan's readers contacted him about an advertisement for "Reno's Pig Palace" that she had seen in an old city directory. Rollan had no idea what the ad referred to, so he put the question in his column. As it happened, I knew that "Pig Palace" was the popular appellation for the Nevada Packing Company, a meatpacking firm which once operated on East Fourth Street. I so informed Rollan. In the course of our correspondence, the matter of anthologizing the Nevada Historical Society's "This Was Nevada" series came up. I told Rollan of our desire to put the articles in a more permanent format. Nothing came of the proposal until Frank Brown of the Society's Docent Council initiated a personal contact between Rollan, myself and Society Director Peter Bandurraga. We had lunch downtown, discussed a possible grant and worked out the details in succeeding weeks.

Rollan and Marilyn typify the best in Nevada's citizenry. Both could have completed their education here and moved on to bigger ponds elsewhere, but they chose to stay, continuing a tradition which has a long and rich history. Nothing compelled George Lovelock to remain in Big Meadows. He would have been an asset to any community. The same was the case with Jeanne Wier. Surely there would have been greater honors in a larger, more prestigious university had she chosen to leave Nevada. Frank Baud, founder of Winnemucca, is another case in point, as is Lem Allen, Churchill County pioneer, Hannah Clapp, pioneer educator, Abe Curry of Carson City, Reno's Myron Lake, W. W. Booth of the *Tonopah Bonanza* and half a hundred others who came to love this rough land.

Like all writers, I am indebted to those who have broken trail in the past, making it easier for those of us still exploring the wilds of Nevada's history. I also feel an obligation to the many readers who have taken it upon themselves to correct my errors of fact or interpretation, suggest new stories or simply call because something I had written stirred a memory or two. There is much to chuckle over in this volume, a bit of sadness and even a touch of anger. I hope everyone finds a little something of interest. Should this volume catch on with the public, it will not be the last.

Introduction

AMONG THE STATES of the nation, Nevada is unique. Even among the states of the West, Nevada is unique. The reasons lie not primarily with her major industries or even her wildly various landscape. It is the history of her people that has made Nevada unique among states. Where the histories of other states fit into a regional context or encompass developments similar to others, Nevada stands alone.

Certainly the land is important in explaining Nevada's past, as well as her present. Stark in its contrasts, the state presents alpine peaks and meadows, crystalline lakes and gushing torrents, high valleys filled with sage and rabbit brush, wide sand stretches and barren *playas*.

Much of the land of Nevada is hard, yielding only a bit in agricultural bounty. Great mineral wealth has come from Nevada, but the human cost has always been equally great. The land of Nevada is a force with which humans have always had to contend. Nothing has ever come easily, and every venture has started with an uncertain outcome.

Many other lands have been tough and difficult, however. The uniqueness of Nevada has come from her people. Many of them came here on their way to somewhere else, pausing only long enough to seek a fortune or just some relief from the rigors of transcontinental travel. Others came to stay—and this remains the case even today—but found they could not surmount the difficulties of life here or for other reasons decided to return home. The result has been a decidedly transient population and often a very small one.

With such a population Nevada has been subject to strong influences from other parts of the country. In the nineteenth century especially, the Southern Pacific Railroad and various mining interests from San Francisco so controlled the political, economic and social life of Nevada that the state appeared to be a colony of

California. John Mackay, one of the Comstock silver barons, is justly revered as a hero in Nevada because he and his family remained to live here and to contribute to the advancement and well-being of the state. Few followed their example in the early days, and Nevada suffered. Her wealth was taken away, and she herself was abandoned when it was gone. Fortunately, that pattern has changed. Nevada's prosperity, even with the economic vagaries common in the closing years of the twentieth century, is stable enough to support an increasingly expanding population.

In 1905 in an address given before a meeting of the Nevada Academy of Sciences, Jeanne Elizabeth Wier, the first director of the Nevada Historical Society, advanced an explanation of the state's development:

> Nevada is scarred, because of the unfavorable geographical condition and because an unusual factor, gold, diverted still more strongly the natural westward development which should have included this section. The population flowed all around it and about it and then when the California trail was opened, directly through it, and left it still an isolated vacant spot. Then a little part of the human mass which had poured by ebbed back into the Washoe District; then came the discovery of gold and silver and the great rush to the Comstock; and then the conferring of Statehood upon this people of abnormal growth. . . . And still the scars remain and always will remain. For it is a scar, not merely of scant population, but of retarded development as well—the scar that comes from the lack of home-building instinct and from the absence of an agricultural stage in its proper time and place. . . . Unfortunate has it been for Nevada that its youth was spent, not under the open skies in closest contact with even a desert soil, but in the depths of the dark mines. Something of the light and joyousness of her life has been sacrificed forever. You can cut your finger and the wound may heal, but, if the hurt be but deep enough, the scar will remain through life.

It may well be that Jeanne Wier's professed preference for Thomas Jefferson's vision of the nation drawing its strength from citizen farmers reveals more of her own origins in Iowa than it does of what happened in Nevada. Nevertheless, her perception that the state has been scarred, that it has lacked something in its history that would make it like other states, is a perception that has been shared by many writers since her time. Up until the end of the nineteenth century, the usual reason given was the obvious effect of the mining industry, not taking into account the benefits the state's preeminent industry brought with it. In the twentieth century, especially since the end of World War II, the gaming industry has taken a goodly share of the blame. Both explanations are obviously simplistic.

Many writers have made serious attempts to examine what might be lacking. Full control of the state's land (the federal government owns eighty-seven per cent of it) remains an often-cited missing element. The ideas advanced earlier in this introduction are all part of the usual explanations. So far no one has come up with a fully satisfactory explanation of what it is about Nevada that seems to be lacking. Whatever it is, it says a lot about what it is that makes Nevada unique. That is what makes the whole question so fascinating.

Those who in recent years have tried to define the region of the West have also had great difficulty in explaining Nevada's unique place. Unfortunately they have too often simply left Nevada out. The task of explaining Nevada, then, has been left to Nevadans. It is no surprise that the best scholarship and writing about the state has been by her native sons and daughters and others who have chosen to spend their lives here. That is not to say many others do not attempt to write about Nevada, hardly the case when so much appears in print about gaming and glitter and crime and nuclear waste and the like. Much of that focus is on the gaudy and the bizarre. It takes a genuine love of the place to understand it and to know the virtues and the faults that are mingled in the tapestry of Nevada's fabric.

There is historic irony in the fact of Nevada's history's having to be written by Nevada's historians. On May 13, 1912, Professor Herbert E. Bolton, the great historian of the West at the University of California, gave an address to the annual meeting of the Nevada Historical Society, which he called, "The Obligation of Nevada Toward the Writing of Her Own History." He began:

> Patriotism, like charity, should begin at home. No doubt the ultimate civic ideal should be a great and exemplary Nation, but nearer home should lie that of making our community and our State worthy members of a great and exemplary Nation. Progress toward this ideal depends upon the arousing of civic consciousness. Underlying civic consciousness is local pride, for pride—

self-pride, self-respect—is the basis for all social as well as of all individual progress, and without it there is no spring to action, no motive to self-improvement. One of the strongest props to individual self-respect is family pride, pride in the worth and works of our ancestors. In the same way an essential element of civic pride is pride and interest in our community's past.

Bolton's presence in Reno that spring evening in 1912 marked a distinguished intellectual heritage for the Nevada Historical Society, for Bolton had taken his doctorate in history at the University of Wisconsin where he had been a student of Frederick Jackson Turner, the author of the famed "Frontier Thesis." It was Turner's view, which he instilled in his many students, that the western frontier was the cradle of the distinctively American character, that under the stress of a difficult frontier environment European immigrants and their institutions were changed into Americans. In Bolton's words again:

It is now recognized that the West has been the real bulwark of democracy in our Nation's development. In the West experiments in democratic government have had their freest trial. The constant return of man on the frontier to primitive conditions, where a man was valued for the power of his strong right arm, where one man was as good as another, if he so proved himself to be, could but engender a race of individualists.

Although modern scholarship has considerably altered its view of the role of the West in national history since Turner's day, few dispute that it needs to be constantly examined and interpreted. Turner's influence, amplified by his many students, has been tremendous.

Jeanne Wier was particularly influenced. She completed a bachelor's degree in history in 1901 at the new Stanford University. There she studied under Turner's close academic friend, Max Farrand. Keeping her association with the California school even as she taught at the University of Nevada, and founded the Nevada Historical Society, she came to know Bolton, who was at Stanford for two years before moving on to Berkeley. It was thus due to Turnerian influences that Jeanne Wier modeled the Nevada Historical Society on the State Historical Society of Wisconsin, a pioneering scholarly institution, located on the campus of the University of Wisconsin in

Madison, and dedicated to collecting material and promoting research on its state and region. Her long tenure as director of the society, until her death in 1950, ensured that Turner's vision would have a shrine in Nevada.

Many historians and others who have written about Nevada have tended to celebrate a romantic image that stems directly from Turner: the hardy and self-reliant frontiersman whose fierce individualism was shaped on the anvil of a harsh and unyielding environment. Twentieth-century writers in particular, looking back at the boom and bust cycles that have continued into the present century from the vantage point of an economy buoyed by casino gaming, have declared that all Nevadans are gamblers, staking everything on uncertain chance. Whether emigrant, prospector, miner, buckaroo, rancher, sheepherder, entrepreneur, promoter or politician, all Nevadans in this view are betting the "come." Nothing is ever certain, and that is the natural order of things.

This view of Nevada's history ignores most women—with the exception of Eilley Bowers, Julia Bulette and Anne Martin. The native Americans are most charitably seen in this view as the unfortunate victims of the inexorable advance of the gamblers. All other non-whites simply do not exist. Certainly there have been, and continue to be, many excellent historians who seek to present historical reality in all of its subtle complexity. There are many whose work today ranks with that of any scholar anywhere. Nevertheless, the myth persists.

The myth will likely change, however, as the character of modern Nevada society changes under the weight of massive immigration from the rest of the nation, especially California, and from the rest of the world. In the face of recent economic dislocations, efforts are underway to diversify the state's economy, inevitably bringing in different people with different attitudes. The state is just beginning to see confrontation on a large scale between older attitudes and the new.

It has become a cliché that California, perched on the Pacific Rim, leads the nation in social trends and experiments. As with all clichés, there is a certain amount of truth in that statement. In reverse fashion, however, Nevada is also on the cutting edge of social change. Mere proximity has closely associated Nevadans with Californians. But here the older, more conservative and stable soci-

ety is better entrenched than in California. It is here in Nevada that
the epic clash between change and continuity in American life is
taking place. With a smaller population, Nevada has conflicts that
are easier to see. They never get lost in the vagueness and ambiguity
of large scale.

Among the community of states, Nevada is comparatively young,
and her written history is rather short. Nevertheless, there has never
been a lack of interest in the state's history. Only resources have
been scarce. The long existence of the Nevada Historical Society
attests to that interest. The society's first publication came in 1907,
three years after its founding. The publication was a selection of
papers on various topics collected together with the society's annual
report. Several similar reports followed. For a while there was little
or nothing done in terms of sponsoring scholarship, but by the 1950s
the spark was rekindled. The *Nevada Historical Society Quarterly*
began publication in the spring of 1957. Various monographs and
reports occasionally appeared. In May of 1975, the series under
consideration here, "This Was Nevada," made its debut. At first
only a few Nevada newspapers gave space to the column in their
Sunday editions. But as the series found popular acceptance, fewer
editors were skeptical. Today "This Was Nevada" appears in nearly
every newspaper in the state.

Dr. John Townley, then the director of the society, wrote the first
few articles. Phillip I. Earl, the society's Curator of Exhibits, was
involved soon after. Over the years several authors on the society's
staff and from outside have contributed their efforts. These include:
Guy Louis Rocha, now Nevada State Archivist; Robert Nylen, now
Acquisitions Registrar in the Nevada State Museum; Richard Datin,
now Curator of the Nevada State Railroad Museum; Mary Ellen
Glass, retired Director of the University of Nevada Oral History
Program; Reno attorney David Thompson; Jim Johnson; Jeff Hunt;
and Paul Strickland. But it is Phil Earl who has carried the over-
whelming bulk of the responsibility for the series and who is identified in the popular mind with "This Was Nevada."

Earl is in many ways ideally suited for his task. Although born in
Utah, he came to Nevada at an early age when his father went to
work on the Boulder Dam project. Raised in Boulder City, he grew
familiar with the surrounding mountains and deserts. He has never
lost his love of exploring Nevada's expanses. A stint in the United

States Army took him to France for two years, an eye-opener for any Nevada boy or girl. After discharge he returned to Nevada, where he took a bachelor's degree in history and political science at the University of Nevada, Reno in 1964. After a few years teaching in Nevada and California, Earl was appointed Curator of Exhibits at the Nevada Historical Society in 1973. A master's degree in history from UNR followed in 1975. He also teaches Nevada history for Truckee Meadows Community College. In addition to "This Was Nevada," Earl is the author of numerous articles and notes in the *Nevada Historical Society Quarterly, Nevada Magazine, The Washoe Rambler* and several other journals.

Earl is not the sort of historian who spends his time on analysis of grand themes. Rather, he is insatiably curious about people—who they are, what they think and what they do. His primary sources have usually been the state's newspapers, often the only source for many of Nevada's now-vanished communities. It is obvious that he is a tireless researcher. Combined with his energy are an easy writing ability and the historian's memory for detail. The result has been a nearly inexhaustible supply of fascinating articles. After more than ten years, the series remains ever-popular; and Earl is widely known for his expertise in Nevada's history.

The present volume is a small selection from the hundreds of stories Earl has written for the series over the years. They are a representative sampling and, taken together, offer the reader serious insight into important aspects of the state's history. The society's Assistant Director and editor, Cheryl Ann Young, has organized the articles into topical sections. A number of historical photographs from the society's collection increase the reader's understanding.

The first section deals with the namesakes of several places in Nevada. Often these were people whose actions—whether they ever set foot in the state or not—had a great effect on Nevadans. The names of other places represent an important reminder of the state's Washo, Paiute and Shoshone heritage. The section on railroading emphasizes an important element in the development of the state, both north and south. The Mormons were the first Anglo-Americans to build settlements in Nevada, and they continue to play an important role in the state's affairs. "Famous Nevadans" celebrates the lives of several individuals who brought fame to the state, either at home or away. They include a singer, a stagecoach driver, a Nobel Laureate, an engineer, a movie star, a painter and financier. Mining was central to the state's economy in the nineteenth century and remains one of the primary industries today. Nevada is, in fact, the leading gold-producing state in the country. The miners' stories are central to understanding the state's birth and growth.

The last two sections present two of Earl's favorite topics—outlawry and prize fighting. Nevada was a part of the frontier and had its share of shootings, hold-ups and lynchings. They provide much of the color Americans have always sought in the West. Beyond color, championship prize fights in Nevada, when they were illegal everywhere else, caused the first national outrage over Nevada's sinful ways. Easy divorce laws and open gaming of course followed. But the Corbett-Fitzsimmons fight in 1897 was the first occasion for Nevada to be castigated on all sides and for her to show her legendary frontier independence.

It is obvious that a great deal of Nevada's history has been left out of this volume. There is nothing here of cowboys, gamblers, urban growth or many other topics. Indeed, over half of Nevada's history is in the twentieth century, and most of the stories are set in the nineteenth. But—with luck—there will be more to come in future volumes.

The fact that this volume is appearing at all is due in large measure to the kind generosity of Rollan and Marilyn Melton of Reno. Their donation has funded publication costs for this collection of *This Was Nevada* and launched a whole new series of publications for the Nevada Historical Society. We are extremely grateful to the Meltons for their "historical consciousness" and their determination to make things happen. We are also grateful to John F. Stetter and his staff at the University of Nevada Press, who have very kindly provided expertise and skill in bringing this project to completion. But above all, this is Phil Earl's book, Phil Earl's Nevada. We invite you to spend some time with him—for your amusement, to learn something, for whatever reason. This is Nevada, and who knows what will happen on the next roll of the dice?

Peter L. Bandurraga

PART ONE

Nevada's Namesakes

Schurz: Namesake for a
Nevada Indian Community

AMONG NEVADA'S TOWNS and cities, none bear a more prominent name than the small Indian settlement of Schurz in northern Mineral County. Located on the ancestral homeland of the Northern Paiutes, the community was founded in 1881 as a station on the Carson & Colorado Railroad, which had a right-of-way across the reservation. Railroad officials adopted the name in honor of Carl Schurz, Secretary of the Interior and administrator of Indian affairs from 1877 to 1881.

Born on March 2, 1829, at Liblar-On-The-Rhine, Germany, Schurz was the son of a village schoolmaster. His parents made every sacrifice to help him achieve his dream of becoming a professor of history. He attended a *gymnasium* at Cologne and became a doctoral candidate at the University of Bonn in 1847. The Revolution of 1848 intervened, however. At the age of nineteen, Schurz was the leader of a student movement, preaching its gospel through the columns of a newspaper he edited and on the streets of German cities.

Influenced by one of the intellectual leaders of the struggle for democratic institutions, Professor Gottfried Kinkel, Schurz became involved in an abortive uprising at Siegburg on May 11, 1849. He took part in rebel battles at Ubstadt and Bruchsal in late June and was one of the defenders of the besieged garrison of Rastatt before its surrender. The young revolutionary and two companions escaped to Switzerland and joined a colony of refugees. When he learned his beloved teacher, Professor Kinkel, had been captured and sentenced to life imprisonment at Spandau Prison near Berlin he returned to Germany and broke him out of the prison on November 7, 1850.

In December of 1850, Schurz moved to Paris, but was expelled by the French government in the summer of 1851 as a "dangerous person." Moving on to London, he became associated with Giuseppe Mazzini and Louis Kossuth, two of the great revolutionary leaders of the democratic movement in Europe. America beckoned, however,

3

Carl Schurz, diplomat, scholar, soldier and statesman for whom
Nevada community of Schurz is named. (Nevada Historical Society.)

and Schurz and his wife headed for the United States in August of 1852. They settled in Philadelphia for a time before moving west to Watertown, Wisconsin where he purchased a small farm.

Schurz became a fierce advocate of the anti-slavery cause and was drawn into the fledgling Republican Party. He campaigned for John Charles Frémont, the party's first nominee for President, in 1856 and for Abraham Lincoln in 1858 and 1860. After Lincoln's election, Schurz was appointed U.S. Minister to Spain. He remained in the diplomatic service less than a year, returning in May of 1862 to accept a commission as a Brigadier-General in command of a division under Frémont. He served at the second battle of Bull Run, Chancellorville and Gettysburg.

After the war, President Andrew Johnson sent him on a visit to the southern states, but his recommendation to grant the vote to former slaves as a condition for the readmission of the former Confederate states did not find favor with the President. Schurz then left government service and became a journalist with the *New York Tribune* in Washington D.C. In 1866, he became editor of the *Detroit Post*, remaining there a year before joining the editorial staff of the *St. Louis Westliche Post*, a German language daily. In 1868, at the age of thirty-nine, he was named to the U.S. Senate by the Missouri Legislature. In Washington, he opposed a plan to annex Santo Domingo, clashed with the supporters of President Grant and worked to create a civil service system. He became known for his attacks on political corruption, but factionalism in the Missouri Legislature led to his defeat when he again stood for office in 1875.

In March of 1877, Schurz joined the administration of President Rutherford B. Hayes as Secretary of the Interior. He is noted in history for his enlightened treatment of the Indians, the development of national parks and his work to preserve the public domain. On July 26, 1880, Schurz paid a visit to the reservation at Pyramid Lake in northern Nevada. He spoke to the Indians on the evils of drunkenness and gambling and related his plans for the establishment of a boarding school on the reservation.

Leaving the Interior Department in 1881, Schurz became the editor of the *New York Evening Post*. He was a contributor to several liberal journals—*Nation Magazine*, *Harper's Weekly* and *Atlantic Monthly*, among others. In later years, he campaigned against the Free Silver Movement, but supported the Anti-

Imperialist Crusade after the turn of the century. He served as an official of the National Civil Service Reform League for several years and took a prominent role in New York politics.

Carl Schurz was also a man of great personal charm and commanding presence, the essence of the soldier, scholar and statesman. Devoted to his family and friends, he was blessed with a lively sense of humor and a talent for the piano. His three-volume memoirs stand today as his major literary achievement, but his *Life of Henry Clay*, published in 1887, has held up well as a historical work. Carl Schurz's long and productive life came to an end on May 14, 1906, and he is buried in New York.

George Lovelock: Nevada Pioneer

GEORGE LOVELOCK, pioneer Nevadan for whom the community of Lovelock is named, was born in Swansea, Wales, on March 11, 1824. In 1847 he married Mary Forest, and several months later the young couple sailed for Australia, a voyage that took over four and one-half months. Their first child, a son, was born aboard ship in the Indian Ocean.

In Australia, Lovelock found employment in the copper mines, but restlessness impelled him to move to California when word of the discovery of gold reached the South Pacific. The couple embarked for the Hawaiian Islands in January of 1850. The family's ship struck a reef seven miles from shore during a storm. While stranded and awaiting a rescue ship, their second child, an infant daughter, died of exposure.

Upon arriving in the islands, Mrs. Lovelock and her son decided to remain there while George made the voyage to the United States. He arrived in San Francisco on April 3, 1850, and found work as a carpenter. After moving to the community of Happy Valley near Sacramento to build houses, he was back in San Francisco in late June to meet his wife and son. They settled in Brown's Valley, then moved to the fledgling camp of Oroville where George constructed the second home built in that area. In September of 1851, his wife gave birth to another son, Thomas, the first white child born in the community. In 1852, the growing family moved to Marysville, and from there to Butte Creek where he established a store and a livery stable. About half a mile south of there he also erected a sawmill, and the community which grew up around the operation took his name.

In the spring of 1855, George Lovelock pioneered a wagon road eastward across the Sierra Nevada to Honey Lake Valley. In addition to hauling freight to the settlers, he took up some placer claims at Meeker's Flat, above Rich Bar and was soon taking out eight to one hundred dollars a day in gold. When the claims played out and his

George Lovelock, namesake of the Nevada community which bears his name. (Nevada Historical Society.)

freighting business no longer was profitable, he sold his California holdings and moved to Nevada. Establishing a ranch at Rocky Canyon, Humboldt County, in 1861, he remained there until he bought 320 acres at Big Meadows in 1866. He paid $2,250 for the land and secured the first water right on the Humboldt River.

In 1867, as the Central Pacific Railroad line was being surveyed across Nevada, Lovelock donated eighty-five acres for a townsite, right-of-way for the railroad and a depot. A community was thus founded and railroad officials gave it the name of the area's leading citizen, George Lovelock himself. He was also promised a block in town, but had to pay $500 for a half-block, upon which he built a hotel. Later in his life, he unsuccessfully contested the railroad's title to the right-of-way and the depot site.

Eight children were born to George and Mary Lovelock before her death in 1872. George remarried, but his second wife drowned in 1889 in a Humboldt River slough which ran near their home. There were no offspring from this second marriage.

Although he worked as a farmer and a rancher, George Lovelock never lost his interest in mining. He not only prospected, but bought and sold mining properties. The discovery for which he is best remembered was at Cottonwood Canyon, a nickel and cobalt property later owned by the American Nickel Company of New York City. Lovelock never attained great wealth from his mining activities, but his insistence on never giving up led to his death in 1907 in his eighty-third year. He had been out prospecting when he came down with a cold. Returning to his home, he contracted pneumonia. In his last delerium, he raved about mining—going down a shaft, candle in hand, to visit his long-ago comrades in Wales, Australia, California and Nevada. The end came the morning of March 21, 1907.

Many descendants of George Lovelock still live in the community which bears his name and there are others in Reno and throughout the state, but the town is best known for the couples who come there to get married and for the stamp collectors who send stamped envelopes every Valentine's Day to have them postmarked "Lovelock, Nevada."

Mahanagos and Montellion Murray Beatty

THE TOWN of Beatty in southern Nye County takes its name from a pioneer settler, Montellion Murray Beatty. His origins are obscure, but he probably settled in Amargosa country in the early 1880s. As the story goes, he wandered in off the desert one day with all his worldly goods packed on two burros. The Paiutes took him in with every expectation that he would remain among them only until he rested, a few days at most, but day followed day and he showed no inclination to depart.

After some weeks, the Indians held a meeting to discuss their paleface guest and decided to ask him to leave. The leader of the group gave him the word, but he lingered on. The Indians then decided to kill him, but he had at least one staunch defender, Mahanagos, the daughter of their leader. It was apparently for her sake that Beatty tarried, and she had given him to understand that he had found favor in her eyes also. The test of her true love was soon to come.

After Beatty had wrapped himself in his blankets and gone to sleep under the stars one night, the Paiutes held another conference and decided to dispatch him to the hereafter without further ado. Mahanagos, meaning "spring of the desert" in English, came to his defense and his life was spared, but only on the condition that he marry her. Beatty was willing and the wedding took place a few days later with all the ceremony the Indians could muster.

Montellion Beatty settled in with his bride, gave up his dreams of mineral wealth and became for all intents and purposes an Indian. Several children came along in later years, and life in that section of Nevada was serene and prosperous for the growing family. A few ranchers migrated to Oasis Valley just to the north in the 1880s and 1890s, and Beatty occasionally helped prospectors lured to the area by the same dreams which had brought him years earlier.

The Amargosa country was swept into the twentieth century when a gold strike was made four miles to the west in 1904. When

Montellion Beatty, pioneer of Oasis Valley and the namesake for the community of Beatty, Nevada. (Nevada Historical Society.)

The Beatty Ranch, c. 1900. Montellion to the rear and Mahanagos standing in the foreground with two of their children. (Nevada Historical Society.)

the camps of Bullfrog and Rhyolite came into being, the community of Beatty was founded as a freighting center for the Bullfrog District. Three railroads reached the town by the fall of 1907: the Las Vegas & Tonopah, the Bullfrog & Goldfield and the Tonopah & Tidewater. Homes, businesses, schools, churches, hotels and theatres soon graced the once wide-open spaces. Montellion Beatty prospered since many of them were located on his land. When a post office was established on January 19, 1905, Beatty became the postmaster, although he could neither read nor write. His assistant, R. A. Gibson, handled the clerical details, however, and Beatty had time to boost for this town which was being touted as "The Chicago of Nevada" by 1907.

On December 13, 1908, Montellion Beatty fell from a wagon and fractured his skull. He died the next day never having regained consciousness. His widow, Maude, as she was called by her white neighbors, lived another fourteen months, passing away in February of 1910. The Bullfrog District was in a serious decline by 1912, but the town of Beatty has become a quiet roadside community at the junction of Highway 95 and State Route 58, a welcomed break in the journey north from Las Vegas. The town which was founded by a man who became a pioneer for love of an Indian maiden is among Nevada's most charming and progressive, the crowning glory of the Amargosa country.

Henderson: Namesake for an Industrial Town

WHO NAMED Nevada's towns? Why? After whom or what? Several bear the names of pioneer founders, mining magnates or Civil War military officers. The unique industrial community of Henderson in Clark County honors Charles Belknap Henderson, a man who played many roles in the course of his long life.

Born in San Jose, California, on June 8, 1873, Henderson was the son of Jefferson Henderson and Sarah Watts Bradley Henderson, eldest daughter of Louis Rice Bradley, Governor of Nevada from 1871 to 1878. He moved to Nevada with his parents in 1876 and attended the public schools in Elko. After attending the University of the Pacific and Stanford University, he received a law degree from the University of Michigan in 1895. Admitted to the Nevada bar in 1896, he set up a law practice in Elko with Judge George S. Brown.

With the outbreak of the Spanish-American War in 1898, Henderson enlisted and became a Second Lieutenant with Troop M, Second U.S. Volunteer Cavalry Regiment, a Nevada unit. Serving at Fort Russell, Wyoming, and Camp Cuba Libre, Florida, Henderson and his comrades were among those who were never called upon to fight. They remained in Florida until mustered out in October of 1898. The troops in several southern camps had been stricken with malaria and typhoid fever and Henderson nearly died of the latter ailment.

In 1901, Henderson became Elko County District Attorney. Three years later he was elected to the Nevada Assembly, serving only one term before winning a seat on the University's Board of Regents in 1907. He remained a Regent for ten years and was considered by many Nevadans to be one of the best ever elected; however, his opposition to the activities of a women's suffrage group on campus in 1914 later returned to haunt him.

Henderson was appointed to the U.S. Senate in 1918 to replace the late Francis G. Newlands, but his bid for election in his own right in 1920 failed. Henderson had the support of the Democratic Party in

Charles B. Henderson, during a tour in Florida as a member of Troop M, Second U.S. Volunteer Cavalry, August, 1898. (Nevada Historical Society.)

the state, but the candidacy of Anne Martin, running as an independent, drew so many Democratic votes that Republican Tasker L. Oddie walked off with the election. As it happened, Anne Martin had been the President of the Nevada Equal Franchise Society and had clashed with Henderson over campus political activity in 1914. The two later became good friends, but Henderson always rued the day he crossed swords with the feisty feminist. Henderson also had an unusual experience just as his term was ending. On March 5, 1921, he was shot by Charles A. Grock at the Senate Office Building. Grock's grievance went back some eighteen years to an Elko case in which he thought that Henderson had not represented him properly. The wound was minor and Henderson returned to Nevada to resume his legal career.

A life-long Democrat, Henderson was appointed to the Board of Directors of the Reconstruction Finance Corporation in 1934. The RFC had been established in 1932 under the Hoover Administration to provide financing for banks and industries needing assistance during the early years of the Great Depression. In 1941, Henderson became the Chairman of the RFC Board.

In July of 1941, six months before Pearl Harbor, the U.S. government authorized the construction of a magnesium processing plant in southern Nevada to be operated by Basic Magnesium, Inc. The Reconstruction Finance Corporation and the Defense Plant Corporation provided the initial funding for the facility, and some 5,000 homes were subsequently built for plant workers and their families. The residential area was known as Basic Townsite until a post office was established in January of 1944. At this time, there was talk of curtailing the production of magnesium since stockpiles of the metal were adequate for the remainder of the war period. Plant officials and civic leaders thus decided to name their town after a man who had not only been involved in the establishment of the plant, but who was also interested in promoting the post-war industrial use of the magnesium complex, Charles B. Henderson.

Nevadans wanted Henderson to retain the industrial toehold achieved during the war, and were concerned about its becoming another ghost town. Their appeal to Senator Patrick A. McCarran, Senator Edward P. Carville, Governor Vail Pittman and a number of political leaders from the western states was ultimately successful, and the community of Henderson remains today as Nevada's only significant heavy industrial area.

At the time of his death in San Francisco on November 8, 1954, Charles B. Henderson was a member of the Board of Trustees of the Western Pacific Railroad, President of the Elko Telephone & Telegraph Company and a Trustee of the Henderson Bank in Elko. The community of Henderson is the only tangible memorial to the man, although many residents of the town have perhaps never known the origins of the name.

The Naming of Winnemucca

WINNEMUCCA is the county seat of Humboldt County and is as charming and progressive a community as any in the state. The name itself has a Paiute origin. As the story goes, the first white trappers to reach the lower end of the Humboldt River in the late 1840s met a young Indian who claimed to be a chief. The young man happened to be in love and Paiute custom dictated that he dispense with one moccasin as a sign that his heart was not free. The white men thus dubbed him "One Moccasin," often using the Paiute word for footware, *mau-cau.* Thus "One-a-mau-cau" became "Winnemucca." The name has also been variously interpreted to mean "bread giver," "the giver" and "the charitable man," but these terms probably refer to Old Winnemucca, as he became known in later years, not to the meaning of the name itself.

Lee Winnemucca, son of Old Winnemucca, verified the one-shoe origin of the name in an interview with a reporter in August of 1887. However, Chief Harry Winnemucca of the Pyramid Lake Paiute Tribe, a great-grandson, has said that family tradition indicates that his ancestor lost a shoe while fleeing from cavalrymen on the Forty Mile Desert.

Whatever the origin of the name, there remains a controversy as to how it came to be attached to the community. One version of the story is that C. B. O'Bannon, an early 1860s mining promoter and nephew of Orville H. Browning, Secretary of the Interior from 1866 to 1869 gave the name to a mining district organized in 1863.

It is also possible that the town's cognomen had its origins with Frank Baud, a Frenchman who migrated from California in 1862 with two of his countrymen, Louis and Theophile Lay. The men had come to work on Joseph Ginaca and Dr. A. Gintz's abortive Humboldt Canal project. In 1863, they built a toll bridge at the present-day site of the Bridge Street bridge and Baud established a trading post. The fledgling community which developed became known as Frenchman's Ford or French Bridge, but Baud preferred the name

Early-day Winnemucca, a Nevada community which carries the name of a Nevada Indian leader. (Nevada Historical Society.)

Winnemucca. It was this name that was adopted when the first post office was established on February 1, 1866, with Baud as the postmaster.

The community was also known as Centerville in 1866 and 1867, an apparent reference to its central location in relation to the surrounding mines, as opposed to the more remote Unionville, the county seat of Humboldt County at that time. The coming of the Central Pacific Railroad led community leaders to hold a public meeting in the fall of 1867 to decide upon an official name once and for all. Local residents decided upon the name Winnemucca and railroad officials agreed with the decision.

The reason for conferring the honor upon the aging Indian is something of a mystery. Old Winnemucca was not overly friendly towards whites who had intruded into his people's ancestral homeland, which was understandable. He had tried to be a voice of reason and caution during the Pyramid Lake Indian Wars in May and June of 1860, but would probably have led the Indians into battle himself had he felt that they could have decisively won the war.

State Archivist Guy Louis Rocha has studied the matter and feels that Old Winnemucca had likely become a friend of Frank Baud's, who had perhaps helped him through an illness of some sort, provided food when his larder ran out or protected him from other Indians. It is for this reason that Rocha believes Baud insisted upon the naming of the post office after the Indian, although French Bridge or Frenchman's Ford were the names commonly used by most people.

In the fall of 1867, Baud either built a new hotel in the community or took over a previous structure and converted it into a hostelry. He named it the Winnemucca Hotel, perhaps another effort to ensure that the community would be named after his putative Indian friend.

Frank Baud is an undeservingly obscure figure in Nevada's history. He was very likely the first white settler in that section of north central Nevada, since he may have been on the scene a short time before the arrival of the Lay brothers. If this is the case, he certainly deserves the same status as Myron Lake, "Father of Reno," and Jim Butler, "Father of Tonopah." If not the first settler, Baud should certainly be recognized for his efforts to see that the name "Winnemucca" became official.

The Naming of Tonopah

TONOPAH, like several Nevada communities, had other names during its early years which were not satisfactory either to the citizens or to officials of the U.S. Postal Department. Originally known as "New Belmont," it soon took the name of "Butler" in honor of the pioneer locater of the mineral wealth of the district. Jim Butler's first find was made on May 19, 1900, but problems with getting a satisfactory assay and Butler's need to put up his hay on his Monitor Valley ranch delayed a formal filing on his claims until August 27. By that time, "Tonopah," a local Indian name, had been chosen as the name for the site of the original claims.

"Tonopah" comes from either the Shoshone (Central Numic) word *to-nuv*, meaning "greasewood," or the Northern Paiute (Western Numic) *to-nav*, also meaning "greasewood," and *pa*, the word for "water" in both dialects. The name has also been interpreted to mean "brush water springs," "greasewood springs," "little water" and "water brush," the latter being the preferred interpretation of old timers of the area.

Jim Butler is said to have spoken the Shoshone dialect and was considered to be a good friend of the Indians. It is quite likely that he conceived the name Tonopah, but the community which developed around the mines in 1901 took his name. The post office, established on April 10, 1901, was Butler also, but the name never caught on. Tonopah was the cognomen popularly used to refer to the community, and those who had occasion to write to local citizens would pen "Tonopah, c/o Butler Post Office, Nevada" on the envelope. When W. W. Booth issued the first number of the camp's pioneer newspaper on June 15, 1901, the banner read *Tonopah Bonanza* rather than *Butler Bonanza*. Editor Booth became postmaster that fall and was a strong proponent of the name "Tonopah." Irritated by letters coming in addressed to the community of Butler, he was moved to comment in the *Bonanza* of January 18, 1902, that

21

Tonopah street scene, April 1, 1901, eleven months after Jim Butler made the original mineral discovery in the district. (Nevada Historical Society.)

there was no such place as "Butler." "It is Tonopah," he wrote, "and Tonopah it will stay."

The Masons of the community organized Tonopah Lodge No. 28, Free and Accepted Masons, in 1902 and nearly every mine or mining company organized that year had the name "Tonopah" somehow associated with the enterprise. When postal authorities elevated Butler to the status of a third-class post office on January 1, 1903, a petition was circulated calling upon them to change the name to Tonopah. Jim Butler said that he had no objection to a name change since he was seeking no personal honors.

In February of 1904, an Assistant Postmaster General wrote to Postmaster Booth suggesting that he circulate a petition to effect the change. In the letter, he pointed out that twenty-six other states had post offices and towns named "Butler." This had become a source of confusion, he wrote, particularly so in the case of Butler, Nebraska, and Butler, Nevada, since many writers, through carelessness, made the "v" which ends the abbreviation of Nevada and the "b" with which the short form for Nebraska ends almost alike. Postal clerks, not being gifted with occult powers, thus made mistakes and caused inconvenient delays in the mail.

Postmaster Booth dutifully circulated the required document in March of 1904, but officials in Washington D.C. did nothing to make the change for another year. In the meantime, the people of Butler mounted a campaign to move the county seat from Belmont to their community. The bill, signed by Governor John Sparks on February 6, 1905, moved the seat of county government to "Tonopah" as of May 1, 1905. Just a month later, March 3, 1905, Booth was informed that the name "Tonopah" would be official as of May 3. The March 11 issue of the *Bonanza* reflected the change, although it had not yet become official, the banner reading "Tonopah, Nye County, Nevada" in place of "Butler, Nye County, Nevada" which it had carried for the past three and one-half years.

Lake Tahoe and the Legacy of a Controversy

FEW OF Nevada's geographical features have had a history of controversy quite like that of Lake Tahoe, which graces the Nevada-California border. Discovered by an exploring party under the leadership of Captain John C. Frémont of the U.S. Topographical Corps on February 14, 1844, it was first called Lake Bonpland. Frémont had considerable respect for Aimé Jacques Alexandre Bonpland, an eminent French botanist who was associated with the great German geographer, Alexander von Humboldt. Charles Preuss, Frémont's mapmaker, showed the lake as "Mountain Lake" on his charts, and Frémont also substituted this name for Bonpland in his reports of 1845–46. Since von Humboldt used the name originally suggested by Frémont, it gained considerable currency in Europe and among academic cartographers. American mapmakers, on the other hand, sometimes used the name "Frémont's Lake" or "Mountain Lake," and an 1849 *U.S. Exploring Map of Upper California* carried no name at all for the lake.

Maps of the 1850s and 1860s carried the designation "Lake Bigler," an appellation affixed to the lake by W. M. Eddy, Surveyor General of California, in honor of Governor John Bigler, California's third American governor, 1851–1856. In the winter of 1852, shortly after taking office, Bigler had led a rescue party into Lake Valley in the Sierra Nevada to bring out a party of snowbound immigrants. Upon returning to Hangtown, he was met by a group of local dignitaries who proposed that the lake be named in his honor. An immigrant guide published in August of 1853 used two names, "Truckee Lake" and "Bigler's Lake," but Milleson's *Map of the Southern and Middle Mines*, 1854, continued to carry the appellation "Mountain Lake" in the old Frémont-Preuss tradition.

With the outbreak of the Civil War in April of 1861, the name "Bigler" became a subject of intense debate. The former governor was an ardent Democrat and a vocal supporter of the Southern Cause on occasion. He was also suspected of being involved in the

John Bigler, Governor of California, 1851–56, for whom Lake Tahoe was officially named. (Nevada Historical Society.)

so-called Pacific Confederacy, a shadowy conspiracy to take California out of the Union. Pro-Union editors demanded "a change from the Secesh appellation" and called for "no Copperhead names on our landmarks for us."

In May of 1863, a writer of a letter to the *Sacramento Union* suggested "Sierra Lake" as a name. The lake should honor no individual, he wrote, at least not a man who had "nothing but condemnation for the glorious defenders of our Government and covert sympathy with treason." The editor added that "Sierra Lake" would do, but suggested that the Indian name, "Teho," would also be appropriate. The editor of the *Marysville Appeal* pointed out that there was already a "Sierra Lake" near Downieville Buttes, but felt that a change in name was indeed justified. Noting the former governor's convivial habits and the inconsistency of naming a body of water for a man who had no use for the stuff, he suggested that the name be "Italianized" to "Lago Beergler," an appellation "which would always stand as a punning allusion to the bilbulous habits which were reputed to characterize 'Honest John' when he was governor of the state." The editor of the *Union* referred to the *Appeal*'s tongue-in-cheek proposal as "unpleasantly suggestive," but allowed as how it might be proper if a lake of beer were discovered.

Other newsmen were also expressing an interest in the name "Tahoe." On June 1, 1863, the *Sacramento Union* noted that the editor of the *Nevada Transcript* of Nevada City was favorably disposed toward a change. "Why the finest sheet of water in the mountains should be named after a fifth rate politician we have never been able to see," he wrote. He concluded with an endorsement of the supposed Indian name, "Poetical name; Indian name; Proper name." The editor of the *San Francisco Republic* agreed. "We like the idea of sweeping such names off the map," he wrote on July 25, 1863. "If permitted to remain, they will give generations to come a bad idea of us today."

At least one Nevada editor, Myron Angel of the *Reese River Reveille*, preferred Frémont's original name for the lake, Bonpland. Angel mistakenly believed that the Frenchman had actually explored the Sierra Nevada and had seen the lake, but the editor of the *Sacramento Union* held out for the new name. Let Bonpland remain on the maps of France, he wrote, and allow John Bigler to change his name to "John Tahoe" if he wanted public honors.

William Henry Knight, a California cartographer, led the revolt against the name "Bigler." In cooperation with John S. Hittell, editor of the *Daily Alta Californian*, the Reverend Thomas Starr King and Dr. Henry DeGroot, a mapmaker and a writer for various publications, Knight began a search for an Indian name. DeGroot had supposedly made a trip to the lake in 1859 where he inquired about the Indian appellation. His guide or one of his informants, perhaps Captain Jim of the Washo tribe, told him the name was *Tah-hoe-ee*, meaning "big lake" or "water in a high place," with the chief accent on the last syllable. DeGroot later claimed that he induced the U.S. Land Office to change the name officially in 1862.

Another version of the naming of the lake comes from an article by Robert G. Dean of Genoa which was published in the *Territorial Enterprise* on February 3, 1870. According to Dean, he and William VanWagner were the owners of the Old Lake House in Lake Valley at the south end of the lake when the Civil War began. As strong Union supporters they began a search for an Indian name and consulted Captain Jim who told them the name was *Tah-oo*, meaning "big water." Judge Seneca Dean communicated this information to the editor of the *Sacramento Union*, and they got a post office established at their place with the name "Taho" in December of 1863.

Professor Alfred L. Kroeber of the University of California considered the Indian name for the lake to be quite proper. He believed the right word to be *Tah-hoe-ee*, meaning "lake" or "big water." According to other linguists, the Washo word for "lake" is *da'au*, or *da'aw*, often pronounced with a "t" sound, with the accent on the first syllable. The name "Lake Tahoe" is thus something of a redundancy, technically "Lake Lake."

In spite of the popularity of the new name, it never appealed to certain people. The editor of the San Joaquin *Republican* once said that the word had a "vulgar significance," and the *Carson Appeal* carried an article in 1875 in which a writer suggested that the word referred to an Indian woman in mourning. In another article two years later, May of 1877, the editor of the Carson City paper declared that the meaning of the word was not known. "It is mock gibber-

A scene at North Shore, Lake Tahoe, c. 1890. While Lake Bigler was the official name at this time, the Indian name was widely used. (Nevada Historical Society.)

ish," he wrote. Sam Clemens, writing as Mark Twain, leveled the unkindest cut of all. Twain, no lover of the Indians, in *The Innocents Abroad*, 1871, called down "sorrow and misfortune" upon the heads of those who promoted the use of the "unmusical cognomen" for the lake. He claimed that the word could never do justice to the lake's varied wonders and magnificent setting. "People say that Tahoe means 'Silver Lake–Falling Leaf,'" he wrote. "Bosh. It means grasshopper soup, the favorite dish of the Digger Tribe—and of the Pi-Utes as well."

The new name also came in for some rough times in 1870 when the California Legislature was considering the naming of the lake. On January 29, 1870, the editor of the *Placerville Mountain Democrat* flatly stated that Tahoe was a renegade Indian who had murdered many whites in pillaging forays on wagon trains, ranches and small settlements. "Was this therefore a logical choice for the naming of those beautiful waters?" he asked. The editor of the *Daily State Register* of Carson City expressed the opinion that Tahoe was an Indian who was disliked even by his own tribe, while John Bigler was a man who had actually rescued a group of white travelers from the very same "thieving Indians." A scribe for the *Truckee Republican* ventured to remark that "Tahoe" was probably the idiomatic Indian word for whiskey, "Big Water."

Politics entered into the legislative debates with the Democrats favoring Lake Bigler in honor of "Honest John," as he was known to many Californians. They claimed that the name "Tahoe" had been borne by a "disreputable and vicious" Indian chief who had murdered an American family by the name of Rothrock on the Truckee River in the early days. Both houses of the California legislature were dominated by the Democrats and on February 10, 1870, a resolution was approved by both houses declaring the lake to be "Bigler" in honor of their fellow party member.

Dan DeQuille of the *Territorial Enterprise* had satirically suggested that the lawmakers take the next logical step and make the writing or uttering of the name "Tahoe" a prison offense. "That would do the business," he proclaimed on February 4. The Nevada writer resented the presumptuousness of the Californians and proposed that the Nevada portion of the lake should have a name selected by the state's own lawmakers.

The name "Bigler" did not return to popular usage. One Californian, referring to the use of Indian appellations for geographical features, remarked that "Their names are on your waters and you may not wash them off." Even so, the official road signs of the California Highway Department for decades did not point the traveler to Lake Bigler, but rather to Lake Tahoe. Finally in July, 1945, the lawmakers finally acted to change the name. The new statute, passed on July 18, read as follows: "The lake known as Bigler shall hereinafter be known as Lake Tahoe."

PART TWO

Tales Along the Tracks: Nevada's Railroads

Railroading Life

RAILROADERS, like all people engaged in dangerous occupations, have been known to have peculiar superstitions. Some engineers believed that it was bad luck to have their engines turned toward the sun when they were sitting in the roundhouse, and others would refuse to take an engine on her maiden run on a Friday. Another prevalent superstition among engineers had to do with the direction their locomotive was rotated on the turntable. Some insisted upon the engine being turned to the right while others demanded a counterclockwise turn, and each group was as adamant as a Baptist minister preaching hellfire and brimstone. Many engineers made a practice of being present to assure themselves that the rotation was done correctly. When asked about this, they could cite numerous accidents which had occurred to engines incorrectly handled in the roundhouse.

Other railroaders had no confidence in a locomotive which had been in an accident. No matter what the condition of the restored piece might be or how easy the run she was assigned to, engineers would have rather gone out on the worst scrap heap in the yard and be assigned to the most difficult run so long as the locomotive had never run afoul of Lady Luck.

There were also those who believed that they would meet misfortunes of all kinds if they should happen to encounter a cross-eyed person on the way to work. If the person happened to be a woman, many engineers would avoid going out on their runs, even at the risk of being "called on the carpet."

Many people have a certain amount of bad feeling about the number "13," but it was the number "9" and its multiples which bothered railroaders. Southern Pacific Engine No. 1266, to cite but one example, was once a "nine-spot." After jumping the tracks numerous times and killing two men, she was renumbered. Few engineers would take her out, however, and she was finally scrapped. Conductors and brakemen also had many superstitions,

Railroaders posed for the camera in Winnemucca, c. 1890. Like many men who followed dangerous occupations, railroaders were a superstitious lot. (Nevada Historical Society.)

as did track layers. If one of the latter should stumble in crossing a rail, he would retrace his steps and cross again to ward off a future disaster.

Colonies of railroad men and their families grew up around division points and terminal headquarters. They seldom mingled with the general populace any more than was absolutely necessary, however, because many "outsiders" had prejudices against them. The phrase "only a railroad man" was given a certain emphasis or inflection which, in the minds of those who kept the trains running, implied a stigma. Landlords, boardinghouse-keepers and other businessmen often looked upon the railroader as easy prey, reason enough to induce a bit of clannishness among them.

With their friends and those of their own kind, railroaders were a happy-go-lucky lot, but were brave to the point of rashness when an emergency called for quick action to prevent a brother from being ground to death or maimed for life. They loved their work and asked for no thanks, medals or rewards for doing it. Indeed, for many it was almost a religious calling. The story is told of an old-time railroader who was finally converted to religion. One evening, he was called upon to lead a prayer. He hesitated a moment, his lips trembling, but finally got control of himself and said in a strong voice:

O, Lord, now that I have flagged Thee, lift up my feet from the rough road of life and plant them safely on the deck of the train of salvation. Let me use the safety lamp known as prudence, make all the couplings in the train with the strong link of Thy love, and let my headlamp be the Bible. And, Heavenly Father, keep all the switches closed that lead off on the sidings, especially those with a blind end. O, Lord, if it be Thy pleasure, have every semaphore block along the line show the white light of hope, that I may make the run of life without stopping. And, Lord, give the Ten Commandments for a schedule, and when I have finished the run on schedule time, pulled into the great dark station of death, may Thou, the superintendent of the universe, say, "Well done, thou good and faithful servant. Come and sign the payroll and receive your check for eternal happiness."

The Big Meadow Valley Washout
of 1907 and 1910

RAILROADS IN NEVADA were always a mixed blessing. They opened up the country, promoted settlement and boomed certain communities, but they often charged extortionate rates, paralyzed local economies through strikes and lockouts and put competing freight outfits out of business. They were also subject to the vagaries of the weather—blizzards, snowstorms, floods, etc.

In turn-of-the-century Las Vegas, the problem was the route of the San Pedro, Los Angeles & Salt Lake line through Meadow Valley Wash, a sixty-mile stretch running south from Caliente to Rox just above Moapa. Engineers predicted floods and washouts for the area when the route was being laid out in 1900 and 1901; however, surveys indicated that it might well be the best of the routes being considered.

By early May of 1905, the railroad was completed and formally opened for business. An auction of townsite lots was held in Las Vegas on May 15 and 16, 1905, and the city was on the map and on the railroad. Less than a year later, March 24, 1906, a rainstorm swept across southern Nevada which lasted four days. It damaged a long stretch of Meadow Valley trackage between Hoya and Minto leaving the line inoperative until April 15.

On February 22, 1907, one of the worst storms in memory struck the area and sent a five-foot wall of water down the wash. The flood took out bridges, ties and rails and scattered timbers all along the right-of-way from Etna to Carp, a distance of some fifty miles. As freight and passenger trains backed up on both sides of the washout, superintendent Van Housen sent 800 men to the scene. Stranded travelers at Etna took over the school for a dance on February 23, and those who found their way back to Caliente attended church services the next day. The community honored its temporary visitors with a dance at the opera house on February 25, and the remainder of the week was taken up with whist parties, pink tea affairs and informal socializing.

36

Flood destruction scene in Meadow Valley Wash, January, 1910. (Nevada Historical Society.)

Up at the washout, life had taken a grimmer turn. At 8:00 A.M. on Thursday, February 28, a flat car loaded with men and timbers backed into a car loaded with heavy ties. Some men jumped just before the impact, but the load of timbers fell on those who could not get off in time. Two men were killed instantly and fifty others were injured, some badly mangled. A relief train set out from Las Vegas with Dr. Roy Martin aboard, and the injured arrived back at Las Vegas at 4:00 P.M. Two more men died on the journey south.

Of those who died at the scene, only one was returned to Las Vegas. The other, an Austrian laborer, had had his head and his legs cut off and was buried on a sloping hillside not far from the scene of his death. The mound of his grave was tenderly patted down by his fellows, and they talked of erecting a monument to the "Unknown Railroader" on the site. A few days later another rain washed away all traces of the gravesite and all the repair work that had been completed.

The people of the community were concerned about a possible food shortage since some bridges on the run in from Los Angeles were also washed out. The last of the community's ham and eggs were gone by March 7, and the chickens were reported to be hiding in the brush. Supplies soon came in from Moapa Valley, however, and there was talk of building a steamship to traverse Meadow Valley between the washed-out sections.

Two Las Vegas men on the repair crew were killed when a crane toppled on March 25, and the line was not finally opened to traffic until April 12. Las Vegans made the best of the situation. The Jolly Dozen Club continued to meet weekly and Las Vegans organized the Help One Another Club. A St. Patrick's Day Grand Ball was held on March 17, and April Fools' Day was also marked by a dance, both sponsored by the Eagles' Lodge. Idle railroaders had meanwhile been occupied with maintenance work on the rolling stock, and some of the laborers had planted flower beds at the Las Vegas depot. The flowers were beginning to bloom by the time the blockade ended, and housewives were soon coming downtown to cut starts for their own gardens.

The 1907 Meadow Valley Wash flood and the blockade of Las Vegas had passed into history by 1910, and most Las Vegans firm-ly believed that their city would never again go through such an ordeal. James Shanahan, the engineer in charge of reconstruction, had checked with residents who lived near the wash and had decided to raise the new grade a full four feet above the 1907 high water mark. He failed to heed the warnings of an old Indian: "Water up here," the old man said as he pointed high up the side of the canyon. "No, no, high water here," the engineer insisted, indicating his own lower estimate.

By early fall of 1907, some 700 men were at work rebuilding the grade through the wash. Seven steel bridges were constructed, the river channel was changed through riprapping and the grade was realigned in several places. The project cost the San Pedro, Los Angeles & Salt Lake Railroad $769,572, and it appeared as though Shanahan had succeeded, but his Irish luck ran out in January of 1910.

An unprecedented set of circumstances led to the flood of 1910. A deep snow covered the hills and filled the gulches and ravines in late December. On December 31, a warm rain began to fall and continued without interruption for the next forty-eight hours. The rain and the melting snow overtaxed the carrying capacity of the wash, and a wall of water fifteen to twenty feet in height thundered down a hundred miles of the tracks battering down bridges and trestles, washing away the carefully sculptured grades and roadbeds.

At Boyd, fifteen miles south of Caliente, the engine and twenty-two cars of a freight train were washed off the track, the crew barely escaping with their lives. Station agents at the lonely points within the wash took to the hills. At Elgin, an agent's wife gave birth to a healthy daughter as she was being rescued from the path of the flood. In Caliente, where the wash widens into an extensive plain, flood waters deposited a foot of silt in homes and completely disrupted operation of the roundhouse and machine shops.

In Las Vegas, the disaster struck just as railroad officials were planning on opening a new machine shop which would mean an additional $50,000 per month payroll. By mid-January, some railroad workers were being laid off or transferred to Los Angeles and Las Vegas was again facing bleak economic times. Soon a debate was underway as to whether to reroute the line out of the wash, but railroad officials decided against a rerouting. Repair work began in early March, and the Las Vegas economy was revived as the community became the supply headquarters for the operation.

One hundred scraper teams and some 1,000 men were on the job

Destruction from the flood in Meadow Valley Wash which struck
the area in February, 1907. (Nevada Historical Society.)

Flood destruction at Caliente, January, 1910. (Nevada Historical Society.)

by mid-March and the number had tripled by early April. Pile driving equipment for bridges and trestles was also brought in and labor shortages became so serious that lawmen in Caliente were talking of "vagging" the town's idlers and pressing them into service. Mexican laborers were finally brought in to relieve the shortage, and the work continued apace.

Las Vegas boomed, but life continued much as before. The Isis Theatre offered new motion picture features weekly, the Las Vegas Gun Club held a prize shoot on February 6, and the ladies of the Eastern Star, the Ladies' 500 Club and St. Agnes Guild continued with bridge luncheons and parties. The Eagles' Lodge sponsored a dance on Washington's Birthday and all attending showed up in colonial costumes. Construction of a new school began in May, and Editor Charles Squires of the *Las Vegas Age* was boosting the organization of a commercial club to promote the community once the rail connections were reestablished.

Repair work was completed in late May and the first through passenger train from Los Angeles arrived at 9:30 A.M. on Sunday, June 11. The entire population turned out at the depot to greet the train, and many people were back at 5:50 that afternoon to meet the first train in from Salt Lake. Seven freight trains rumbled through town the next day and laid-off workers were soon being rehired as the new shops opened. The temporary repairs were replaced by a new high line through Meadow Valley Wash in 1912 and it lasted until another flood in March of 1938 tied up the line for three weeks.

The Las Vegas Railroad Strike of 1922

AMONG THE PROBLEMS encountered by the citizens of Nevada's railroad towns in the early days were labor disputes. The people of Reno, Wadsworth, Winnemucca and Elko had had their troubles with the famed American Railway Union Strike in 1894, and Las Vegans went through much the same travail during a nationwide railroad strike in the summer and fall of 1922.

The San Pedro, Los Angeles & Salt Lake line through Las Vegas was taken over by the Union Pacific in May of 1921. Whereas officials of the original line had had a good relationship with the people of Las Vegas, Union Pacific officials were concerned solely with revenue. Several months after the takeover, the shop crews were thinned out and sixty men lost their jobs. A strike was considered, but the walkout was delayed pending negotiations. Although talks took place, there never was a satisfactory resolution and feelings toward railroad officials were still bitter when the nationwide dispute came to a head in July of 1922.

The 1922 strike originated with the government takeover of the railroads during World War I. Wages and working conditions were negotiated through governmental boards to keep the trains running, and the Transportation Act of 1920 established the Railroad Labor Board to maintain peace in the labor ranks. Railroad officials claimed that wages had gone too high during the war, and they got no relief when the board granted the shopcrafts a twenty-two percent increase in July of 1920. President Warren G. Harding assumed office in 1921, and appointed men to the board who were sympathetic to management. A twelve percent wage reduction was made in July of 1921. A strike might have followed if the engineers, firemen, brakemen and conductors had not been able to get some concessions.

A second wage reduction on June 5, 1922, resulted three weeks later in a nationwide strike of shopmen and maintenance-of-way employees. Reports of scattered violence in other parts of the coun-

Las Vegas, mid-1920s, about the time that a violent labor dispute disrupted the otherwise peaceful community. (Nevada Historical Society.)

try soon began to come in, and the various railroads were reported to be hiring guards and workers to replace those on strike—"scabs" in the popular parlance of the time. These reports were probably exaggerated by railroad officials in hopes that state officials would call out the National Guard to break the strike.

Las Vegas was quiet but railroad electricians walked out soon after the shopmen, leaving the city in darkness since the Union Pacific furnished power to the community through the Consolidated Power & Telephone Company.

E. E. Calvin, Union Pacific superintendent in Salt Lake City, was meanwhile building up petty incidents into major confrontations and requesting Governor Emmet D. Boyle to send the State Police. Union leaders denied that there was any trouble, as did Dan Ranear, a State Police Inspector posted to Las Vegas by the governor shortly after the strike began. This temperance was soon to change.

On July 12, at 3:00 A.M., seven men were taken off the train on the edge of town and escorted back to the California line. Governor Boyle was immediately informed, and he sent word to Ranear that a repeat of the incident would bring in the State Police. Railroad officials fenced off the yard, stationed armed guards inside and moved workers and their families inside. Picketing strikers continued patroling outside the "stockade" until a federal injunction on July 28 limited their numbers to two men.

On August 3, the wife of a railroad foreman taking lunch to her husband was attacked by four wives of striking shopmen as a crowd looked on. Later that evening, trainmaster George A. Zentmayer was abducted, taken to the edge of town and given a bath in heavy fuel oil. Boyle offered a $1,000 reward for the apprehension of those responsible.

Meanwhile Superintendent Calvin was keeping up a steady stream of requests for action, and Governor Boyle decided to go to Las Vegas to investigate. Arriving on August 12, the day after the engineers, firemen, brakemen and conductors walked out and shut down the line entirely, he consulted with local officials. As if by design, at 10:45 P.M. the next evening, shooting broke out at the yards. What happened is not known but one striker drew a gun on the governor. He dropped it when told to do so, but the governor decided then and there to call in the State Police. He took a hand personally in rounding up eighteen other armed men that night, and the situation quieted markedly when the first sixteen troopers arrived on August 16.

With negotiations to settle the strike proceeding, both sides in Las Vegas settled down to wait. On September 2, State Police troopers arrested six men in the town's red-light district. Ranear claimed that they were I.W.W. radicals, drug addicts and vagrants whom local lawmen were ignoring, but the citizens resented the interference in local affairs. Half of the sixteen-man contingent were recalled to Carson City three weeks later, leaving only four by mid-October.

The railroad employees and their families fell upon hard times as local merchants and landlords became increasingly reluctant to extend further credit. To raise money, some of the men and their families organized a drama troupe and staged the play "In Plum Valley" at the high school on September 29. Miss Ruth Ingram did a reading from "Peck's Bad Boy" between the acts, Jose Rosi performed on the piano accordion and Mrs. Ruth Young and her daughters sang for the large crowd.

All involved were becoming weary of the strike and a wage settlement was reached in October, but many of the men lost their seniority and other benefits. The strike generally rebounded against the unions involved, and they subsequently lost members and a measure of their power. As for the State Police, their "occupation" of Las Vegas, such as it was, came to an end on December 1 when Governor Boyle ordered the last contingent back to Carson City. The strike soon passed out of the news, and life returned to normal in Nevada's railroad towns.

Theodore Judah: Railroad Builder

IT TOOK MORE than steel rails to link the Pacific and Atlantic coasts in the nineteenth century. It took men of steel, vision and courage. Such a man was Theodore Dehone Judah, "Crazy Judah" as he was known because of his single-minded interest in pushing a railroad across the Sierra Nevada in the 1850s and 1860s.

A graduate of Rensselaer Polytechnic Institute of Troy, New York, Judah had been associated with the New Haven, Hartford and Springfield Railroad and the Connecticut Railroad before moving to California in 1854 to oversee the construction of a railroad from Sacramento east to Folsom. When the Sacramento Valley Railroad project was completed in 1856, it became the first operating line in the state. The constant sight of the Sierra Nevada to the east intrigued the young engineer. "He seemed to become possessed with the problem," a contemporary writer later wrote of him. "It was almost as if he were crazy."

In 1857, Judah was hired to survey a wagon road across the Sierra and he laid out a proposed route, but he continued to smell the smoke and hear the whistles of locomotives and was soon fired by his employer. For the next four years Judah and his long-suffering wife spent the majority of their time in the Sierra, but the political climate in the country was not right for any large-scale transcontinental railroad project. Southern representatives in Congress wanted a southern route with a western terminal at San Diego or Los Angeles and opposed any notion of northern and central routes through the free states. The project thus had to await the coming of the Civil War in 1861 and the departure of the Southerners from Washington.

In September of 1859, Judah attended the Pacific Railroad Convention meeting at San Francisco to argue for his dream. No financial plan was forthcoming, although he made his point of the necessity of having a railroad span the continent and was able to display the survey he had been working on. He traveled to Washing-

Theodore Judah, pioneer Jewish engineer who surveyed the original route through the Sierra Nevada later taken by the Central Pacific Railroad. (Nevada Historical Society.)

ton D.C. four months later to try to persuade Congress to come up with some money and made friends with a sympathetic Illinois Congressman, John D. Logan, who secured him a room at the Capitol to display his maps, surveys and reports. These were perilous times, however, and Judah returned to California as the Civil War approached.

The young engineer returned to the Sierra in the fall of 1860 and took up with Daniel W. Strong, a self-styled doctor and surveyor who had an interest in railroads almost as fervent as Judah's. Together they set out on horseback to lay out a practical route over the granite Sierra barrier and were gazing down from Donner Summit looking east a month later. Back at Strong's drugstore at Dutch Flat, Judah drew up papers for the Dutch Flat–Donner Summit Railroad Company, but his reputation of being "a little touched in the head" made a joke out of his early efforts to raise money to pursue his dream.

Fortune smiled on Judah, however, when he met two successful Sacramento hardware merchants, Collis P. Huntington and Mark Hopkins. Huntington rounded up others who might be interested in Judah's project, among whom were Sacramento grocer Leland Stanford and Charles Crocker. Together they pledged $35,000 for an initial survey which Judah and his wife carried out during the summer and fall of 1861.

Back in Washington D.C. that fall, Judah was able to pull strings in high places to get himself appointed Secretary to the Senate Committee on Railroads. With the Civil War underway, the transcontinental railroad was now considered a military necessity as well as a political move to keep California and the other western states in the Union. President Lincoln favored the project, and he signed the Pacific Railroad Bill on July 2, 1862, after several months of heated debate in both houses of Congress.

Differences between Judah and his partners soon developed over Judah's feelings that they were more interested in building their fortunes than a proper railroad, and both sides resolved to buy the other out. When he left for New York City in September of 1863 to seek financial backers, he had a $100,000 offer from the Big Four for his stock, but the issue became moot when he contracted yellow fever while crossing the Isthmus of Panama and died in New York City on November 2, 1863.

Had Judah lived and succeeded in taking over the Central Pacific Railroad, the history of western railroading might well have been considerably different. Nevertheless, the substance of his dream did indeed come true and the Central Pacific and Union Pacific lines were joined on May 10, 1869, at Promontory Point, Utah some seven years after his death. Judah might well have been "crazy," but his particular madness inspired one of the world's technological marvels.

At the California Railroad Museum in Sacramento, there is a statue of Judah, but for those who love the railroads, the line across the Sierra Nevada is tribute enough.

PART THREE

The Mormons in Nevada

The Mormons of Carson Valley

BRIGHAM YOUNG and his Latter Day Saints arrived in Salt Lake Valley in July of 1847 with visions of establishing an empire that would be economically self-sufficient while at the same time expansive enough to take in the thousands of new converts they believed would be coming from the eastern states and Europe. In 1849, Young outlined his territorial ambitions in his proposed "State of Deseret" with ideas of exploration as far south as the Gulf of California.

The Utah Territory, created in 1850 with Brigham Young as the political head, was somewhat more restricted in size than his "State of Deseret." Mormon colonies were soon established throughout the area that church officials had previously hoped to include within their domain. Four of these colonies were within the present state of Nevada: Carson Valley, Las Vegas, the Muddy River Valley and Meadow Valley.

Historians have long assumed that these colonies were part of a "master plan," an "outer cordon" of settlements whereby Mormon officials intended to control the American West. Colonies were established for a variety of reasons and with varying degrees of official approval and support, but recent research reveals that there was no such elaborate plan.

The best example of what looks like an "outer cordon" settlement is Carson Valley in western Nevada. The area was within the political boundaries of the Utah Territory, but church officials gave no support or recognition to the Mormons there until January of 1854, almost four years after the first church members arrived. Sam Brannan, the California Mormon leader, visited the area in the spring of 1847 and members of the Mormon Battalion followed in the fall after their discharge from military service in California. Other Mormons traveling to California also passed through Carson Valley, as did thousands of non-Mormons bound for the Golden State, but

53

Genoa, a Mormon fort, constructed by Salt Lake merchants John and Enoch Reese in 1851. (Nevada Historical Society.)

there was no pressing need for a church colony on that end of the Territory.

The discovery of gold in California in 1848 drew some Mormons across the Sierra, although church officials discouraged such ventures. Among those who caught gold fever were fifteen men who set out from Salt Lake in April of 1850. Venturing as far west as Carson Valley, eight of them decided to remain and develop a way-station for trading with passing immigrants. They did not set up shop as representatives of the Mormon Church and there is some question as to whether several of the men were even church members. The leader, Joseph DeMont, was probably a Mormon, but Hampton S. Beatie and Abner Blackburn along with the five other men are believed to have been non-Mormons. The men did a brisk business over the course of the summer, but returned to Salt Lake in October.

John and Enoch Reese were Mormon merchants who learned of the opportunities on the western end of the Territory from Beatie and decided to locate a trading post there. Mormon Station was founded in July of 1851, again without church sanction or involvement of any kind. The Reese brothers prospered and both Mormon and non-Mormon settlers began to take up land nearby, but isolation from centers of civilization and friction between Mormons and their neighbors led to efforts to have the area annexed to nearby California. Carson Valley, in political terms, was an extension of Millard County, Utah Territory, until Carson County was created in January of 1854. Territorial officials hoped that the act would bring about some political stability and help maintain Mormon control of the area; however, effective government did not come until Probate Judge Orson Hyde arrived in June of 1855.

Hyde had a boundary survey conducted and arranged for the election of county officials, but the election of virtually the entire Mormon ticket upset the valley's non-Mormons and led to charges of fraud. Hyde experienced increasing problems in carrying out his judicial duties, and the settlement of more gentiles in the valley threatened what slim control the Mormons had. Another California annexation move in January of 1856 induced Hyde to deliver an ultimatum to church authorities either to send more Mormon settlers or give up the effort in Carson Valley. As President Young was favorably inclined, Hyde sent out an expedition in March of 1856 to explore the valleys to the north: Eagle Valley, Washoe Valley and the Truckee Meadows. On April 6, 1856, church officials decided to accede to Hyde's wishes, and the first parties began arriving in June to take up land in Carson Valley and in the areas to the north.

The settlers had been selected carefully—butchers, weavers, brickmakers, mechanics—some indication that the Mormons intended to establish economic as well as numerical dominance. Hyde's problems were not over; many Mormons were falling away from church teachings and even the missionaries who came fell upon evil ways. The non-Mormons were even more hostile when another county election in August of 1856 resulted in only three of their number being elected, all friends of the Mormons.

The first organizational meeting for the establishment of a stake was held on September 28, 1856. In November, Orson Hyde was called back to Salt Lake and replaced by Chester Loveland. Both men called for more colonists but none were sent. Relations between the Mormons and their neighbors began to improve under Loveland's leadership, and the discovery of gold in Gold Canyon and along the Walker River stimulated the economy. In April of 1857, all the settlers got together to decide upon a new wagon road to California which would add to the prosperity of the valley in the future. Crops were flourishing and new homes were going up, but the end of the Carson Valley Mission was soon to come.

Relations between Mormon officials and non-Mormon federal authorities in Utah had never been good. Exaggerated reports that the people of the Territory were in a "state of rebellion" during the summer of 1857 led President James Buchanan to dispatch federal troops to uphold the authority of the government. On September 5, 1857, word of the trouble reached the settlers of western Utah Territory, and they were ordered to dispose of their holdings and return to Salt Lake forthwith. Parties were dispatched to California to purchase guns and ammunition while those who remained in the valley were trying to sell their farms and get packed up. A few Mormons stayed, but most left for Salt Lake on September 16, one party reaching the Mormon capital on October 25 and the other on November 3. As it happened it was all for naught since church officials had come to an accommodation with federal authorities.

It is one of the many ironies of history that the Mormon settlers of Nevada, for the most part, gave up their land and property and returned to Salt Lake City not knowing that their sacrifice would be in vain. Had they stayed in Nevada, the Mormons would likely have had a much more prominent role in the state's early history.

The Las Vegas Mission

THE MORMON MISSION at Las Vegas has a better claim as an "Outer Cordon" settlement than does Carson Valley, but an investigation of the rationale for its establishment might lead the conscientious scholar to a different conclusion. The Las Vegas Mission was part of the second phase of Mormon colonization from 1850 to 1856. Colonies were founded at Parowan and Cedar City, Utah (1850), San Bernardino, California (1851), Fort Supply (1853), Moab, Utah (1855), Lemhi, on the Salmon River in northeastern Idaho (1855), Las Vegas (1855) and Fort Bridger, Wyoming (1856). Drawing lines to connect these points on a map encloses an expanse of territory that is about one-sixth of the land area of the U.S.

Las Vegas Springs became a resting place on the Old Spanish Trail in 1830 and was traveled by explorer John C. Frémont in 1844. Mormon trailblazer Jefferson Hunt led a party through the area in the fall of 1847, followed by Mormon leader Parley P. Pratt who conducted an expedition to explore the trail from Salt Lake to southern California in late 1849 and early 1850. Pratt's men investigated the topography of the land, mineral resources, grazing possibilities, water supply, vegetation, timber resources and favorable locations for future settlements. The iron deposits at Iron Mountain discovered by the Pratt expedition led to the establishment of Cedar City in 1850 and San Bernardino in 1851.

The trail south had become known as the "Mormon Corridor" by 1851, and some twenty-seven Mormon communities including Las Vegas were established along the route by 1855. Las Vegas was surely a critical juncture on the trail, but there were other reasons for the establishment of a mission there. Investigation of the records indicates that the primary motive was an interest in doing more missionary work among the Indians. Continued Indian trouble which culminated in the Walker War of 1853 made church leaders realize that greater efforts must be made to civilize and proselytize the "Sons of Laman," as the native Americans were called. The

A scene at Las Vegas's old Mormon Fort, 1911. (Nevada Historical Society.)

effort among the Indians was also a part of the so-called Mormon Reformation which involved the establishment of schools and a rededication to the Mormon faith.

At a general conference of the church held in Salt Lake in April of 1855, some 300 missionaries were challenged to establish new settlements or reinforce older ones. Of this number, thirty men were chosen to establish a mission at Las Vegas.

The first party reached Las Vegas Springs—"a nice patch of grass about a mile wide and two or three miles long," as George W. Bean described it—on June 14 and the remainder arrived the next day. The men set about preparing a campsite and began to lay off plots of land for fields. Brother Rufus Allen led an expedition to the Colorado River on June 18, and some thirty Indians from Snow Mountain came for a visit the next week. Realizing that the Indians had been treated badly by whites in the past, the Mormons assured them that they would not be harmed. The missionaries offered to help them with food and encouraged them to attend meetings and learn something of the Mormon religion. The Indians seemed willing to "bury the past" and trust this new group of white men, but Indian thievery of crops and livestock was a problem which was never adequately dealt with during the year and a half that the Las Vegas Mission was in active operation.

The first group of Indian converts, fifty-six men and women, were baptized on November 3, 1855. It would be facile to claim that all the Indians accepted Mormonism simply because they were treated well and were given food in exchange for labor. This was certainly the case with some since life on the desert was hard and they were often on the verge of starvation, but only a cynic would deny that others came over out of genuine conviction.

The Mormons erected a large adobe fort, constructed cattle corrals, put in an irrigation system and built roads. In addition they developed timber sources twenty miles to the north, established a farm for the Indians two miles north of the mission and carried out an extensive exploration and mapping project. They also organized the "Las Vegas Guards," a military unit, and the "Las Vegas Lyceum," a forum for lectures and philosophical discussions.

As the months passed life became tedious and wearing. The men would snap at one another over small incidents and would carry grudges for months over some unintended slight. The fact that the men were sent to Las Vegas without their families was surely a factor in their discontent, although the men went back and forth to Utah on occasional "family leaves."

The crops varied as much as moods. The melons and grain planted that first summer did well, but a hard frost in November killed the grape vines. Worms ate the corn the frost did not take, but there were potatoes and other vegetables in abundance as well as fruit and figs. An experimental cotton crop was harvested in November of 1855 and new grape cuttings from San Bernardino were planted in March of 1856, but the Las Vegas Mission never became self-sufficient. Flour and other necessities were brought from San Bernardino and Cedar City periodically throughout 1855 and 1856.

An additional twenty-nine men were called to the Las Vegas Mission in February of 1856, and a few brought their families. The presence of women and children added a little spice to an otherwise drab existence, but caused some problems as well. Young boys got in fights with Indian youngsters and sometimes drew their parents into the squabbles. On August 19, 1856, the wife of Elijah K. Fuller gave birth to a daughter, the first white child born in that remote outpost. A month later the first school was started.

In March of 1856, John Steele discovered an outcropping of lead and galena at Potosi Mountain some thirty-five miles to the south. Once samples were sent to Brigham Young, an exploring party under the leadership of Nathanial V. Jones was dispatched to Las Vegas. After an examination of the site, Jones returned to Utah to organize a mining company. Brigham Young supported the enterprise, but his decision had an impact on the Las Vegas Mission which could not have been foreseen. William Bringhurst, President of the Mission, was ordered to supply men and provisions for Jones, but he raised some objections and claimed that he had hardly enough food for his own men. A mining mission was organized, however, and a blast furnace was completed in September, but technical problems limited production for three months.

The problems between Bringhurst and Jones had demoralized the missionaries at Las Vegas, and there were meetings on the subject of the nature of the southern effort: Indians or minerals. Bringhurst was disfellowshipped in November, but Brigham Young had already dissolved the Indian mission by that time and released the men from their obligations. A few remained, but most were gone by the end of the year. Jones' mining enterprise was shut down in late January of 1857 after producing less than five tons of lead, and most of the miners were back in Utah by early spring.

Upon reflection, it seems that the Mormons gave up too easily in Las Vegas. Yielding to adversity rather than persevering is not the Mormon style, yet here we have a situation in which there was a chance to establish a permanent settlement, but they gave up. Perhaps Las Vegas deserves more study.

Callville:
Mormon Seaport on the Colorado River

THE FAILURE of the Mormon mission at Las Vegas in 1856 did not discourage church officials, and there was renewed interest in what is today southern Nevada in the late 1850s and early 1860s with the settlement of Callville. Also known as Call's Landing and Fort Callville, this Mormon seaport on the upper Colorado River was the only outlet in the otherwise landlocked state of Nevada.

Brigham Young's proposed State of Deseret of 1849 included the upper Colorado River and there was discussion of using water transport to bring church converts directly from Europe and to facilitate foreign commerce. A trip from the Missouri River to Salt Lake Valley was over 2,000 miles through hostile Indian lands, but the journey from the Colorado River to Salt Lake was only 450 miles through country which would soon be dotted with Mormon settlements. Church officials were also interested in diversifying Utah's economy and planting settlers where crops requiring a longer growing season could flourish—cotton, sorghum, sugar cane, tobacco, grapes, etc. Mining was beginning to spread throughout southern Nevada and northern Arizona in the early 1860s, and church officials came to believe that gentiles would soon take up lands in the surrounding valleys if Mormons did not act to preempt them.

With the outbreak of the Civil War in 1861, church authorities saw an opportunity to engage in the production of cotton as a cash crop, and so the Dixie Mission at St. George was established in October of 1861. The settlers found that they could grow cotton and get it to market profitably. Since the war in the eastern states made the wagon journey west more difficult and held up progress on the transcontinental railroad, church officials began to reconsider the earlier scheme of using the river for commercial and immigration purposes.

An expedition under the command of Lieutenant Joseph C. Ives in 1857 and 1858 determined that the river was navigable. By the summer of 1864 steamship service as far north as Hardy's Landing

Anson Call, Mormon frontiersman and Colorado River pioneer for whom Callville Bay on Lake Mead is named. (Nevada Historical Society.)

The remains of Fort Callville, Mormon seaport on the Colorado
River, c. 1924. (Nevada Historical Society.)

had been established and in June, church officials in St. George appointed a group of men to explore and lay out a direct wagon route to the river and select a site for a port. Four months later, Anson Call was selected to head the party.

Call and his companions went down the Muddy River to its confluence with the Virgin and then on down the Colorado to Hardy's Landing. Two weeks later on December 17, 1864, Call and his men selected a site for the port and warehouses three miles upriver from Las Vegas Wash.

Returning to St. George, Call engaged several laborers for the construction project and purchased the necessary supplies and tools. The first stone warehouse, a few dwellings and several corrals were completed at the site in February of 1865. Church officials were meanwhile making preparations to send settlers to the Muddy country to the north, and others were dispatched to Callville to lay out fields and establish a community.

The plans of church officials for use of the Colorado River never quite came to fruition. After the Civil War came to an end in April of 1865, construction on the Union Pacific Railroad resumed in July. The first steamer, the *Esmeralda*, did not reach Callville until late October of 1866, but service was more or less regular for the next two years. The famers of the Muddy Valley were able to ship cotton to San Francisco and bring in a variety of goods which were difficult to procure otherwise, but no immigrants from Europe were ever routed up the river. Mormon authorities at Salt Lake had considered building a railroad from St. George to Callville, but the completion of the transcontinental railroad in May of 1869 ended whatever economic justification there might have been to continue the steamship enterprise.

Salt Lake entrepreneurs who had financed the warehouses at Callville did not get an adequate return on their investment. Merchants who ordered goods brought in by steamer found that the transportation into Utah was slow and expensive, thus they went back to dealing with overland freight companies. Callville, like the settlements of the Muddy Valley, was within the area transferred from the Arizona Territory to the State of Nevada in 1866. The proprietors of the shipping enterprise would thus have been subject to high Nevada taxes, just as the settlers of the Muddy were, so the business might well have been abandoned even if the railroad had not come along.

Over the years, the abandoned warehouses slowly filled with sand, their significance all but forgotten because of the isolation of their location. With the completion of Hoover Dam at Black Canyon some twelve miles to the south in 1935, Lake Mead began to fill and the old port was covered by several feet of water by the spring of 1938. During subsequent low water periods, the ruins have sometimes risen out of the lake, but the completion of Glen Canyon Dam upstream on the Colorado River in recent years has somewhat stabilized the lake level and old Callville has not been seen for some years.

The Muddy Valley Mormon Colonies

THE MORMON COLONIES of the Muddy Valley, in present-day Clark County, were a part of a new phase of Mormon settlement undertaken in the late 1850s and early 1860s. The colonies of St. Thomas, St. Joseph, West Point and Overton were established when thousands of new converts began to converge upon Utah.

Exploring parties from Parowan and Cedar City in Utah had previously surveyed the Santa Clara and Virgin River Basins before the Civil War broke out in 1861 and induced Mormon authorities to take an interest in the production of cotton. Several small cotton-producing colonies in southern Utah were expanded, and Santa Clara and St. George were established in 1861 and 1862 respectively. Cotton was bringing $1.24 a pound by 1864, with Mormon jobbers developing good markets in the eastern states, thus the interest in settling the Muddy and increasing production. Church authorities also planned the communities as relay points for the new converts arriving at Callville, the projected seaport on the upper Colorado River.

Construction of the first warehouses at Callville began in December of 1864 and the first colonists arrived at what would soon be St. Thomas on January 8, 1865. Others followed and there were forty-five families there by April 1. St. Joseph was established twelve miles upstream in May of 1865 and Mill City, a mill town, was founded in the late fall. West Point on the upper Muddy was settled in 1868 and Overton in 1869.

Life on the Muddy involved unbelievable hardships and privations. Marauding Indians who ran off cattle and stole crops were a constant concern. The Indians were widely scattered and organized into separate small bands, each with its own leadership, thus making it difficult to get the leaders together and negotiate better relations. As time passed conditions improved, but a man could never feel comfortable about leaving his family unprotected or going out without a gun.

The descendants of St. Thomas's pioneer Mormon settlers gathered in front of the post office in 1929. (Nevada Historical Society.)

The Muddy Valley was also infested with malaria-carrying mosquitoes and hordes of grasshoppers, but the chief source of misery for the colonists was the heat during the summer when the temperature could soar to 125 degrees in the shade. "When warm weather came, we were unable to sleep in the house," one man later recalled, "and were compelled to resort to the sheds and sleep on top of them to keep from scorpions, tarantulas, rattlesnakes etc." He also remembered roasting onions and eggs by burying them in the hot sand and cooking carrots simply by watering them in the morning and pulling them out of the ground at noon.

Building materials were so scarce that dwellings were constructed of rough adobe with crude thatched roofs. The settlers were isolated from markets for their crops and from sources of anything that they could not make themselves. Fortunately the settlers had a variety of artisans on hand including blacksmiths, millers, carpenters and masons, as well as teachers and musicians.

For entertainment the settlers held dances, and a man who could play the fiddle was someone of importance. Other civic occasions, such as the July 24th celebration of the day the Mormons arrived in Salt Lake Valley in 1847, were marked by flag raisings, orations, band concerts, races and community dances. In addition, each settlement had its own Mutual Aid Society to promote interest in debates, spelling bees, math contests and other activities which promoted intellectual life.

Economically, the colonies of the Muddy Valley were a mixed success. Some 5,000 pounds of cotton were harvested in 1865, but the end of the Civil War caused prices to fall. Production more than doubled in 1866 and 1867, but low prices and high transportation costs kept profits down. Some trade in foodstuffs with the mining camps of Meadow Valley and El Dorado Canyon was beginning in the late 1860s and salt was provided for milling operations, but the poverty and hardships were unending. Only the dedication of the Mormons to their ideals enabled them to hang on for as long as they did.

Ultimately, it was the allocation of the Muddy colonies to Utah, Arizona and Nevada that led to their demise. The creation of the State of Nevada in 1864 placed several areas of Mormon interest outside of church control. A territorial addition to Nevada to the east and the south in 1866 encompassed the Muddy Valley. Nevada officials came in to collect taxes insisting on gold and silver, but the colonists refused to pay. The Utah Legislature created Rio Virgin County in February of 1869 to give the colonists some legal support; however, an 1870 survey revealed that the colonies were indeed in Nevada. Nevada officials filed suit for back taxes in 1870 and refused to give credit for payments already made elsewhere. Brigham Young had visited the Muddy in 1870 and had learned of the difficulties of life there, but it was the boundary and tax situation which finally led him to release the Mormons from their obligations on December 14, 1870. By February of 1871, more than 600 Mormons from the Muddy Valley were once again in exodus, leaving behind 150 homes, 500 acres of cleared land, 8,000 bushels of wheat ready for harvest and an irrigation system valued at $100,000. "Their heart was not in the mission," Joseph W. Foote, colony leader, later wrote. "They hailed with delight anything that would be calculated to release them. . . ." Foote left too, leaving behind his fine vineyard.

Panaca: Meadow Valley Mormon Outpost

MEADOW VALLEY, the location of Panaca, was explored and brief-ly settled by Mormons in 1858 when Brigham Young and other leaders of the church were considering the abandonment of Salt Lake Valley because of problems with federal officials and the pres-ence of U.S. troops. Church officials were able to make an accommodation with the federal government, however, and further settlement in Meadow Valley was delayed until May of 1864.

Panaca, like the colonies of the Muddy Valley, was originally something of an adjunct to the Dixie Mission at St. George, Utah Territory, and was established because church officials felt that a settlement at Meadow Valley would open up additional lands for farmers coming into southern Utah. General Patrick Connor and his "Army Prospectors" had previously made a minerals survey of the area which stimulated interest in the development of mining. Presi-dent Erastus Snow of the Dixie Mission believed that mining would provide support for a community, but he warned the settlers not to be "overcome by the spirit of covetousness, and a desire for riches." He need not have concerned himself. The later mining operations were owned by gentiles, and the Mormon settlers of Meadow Valley never made anything beyond a modest, frugal living. They once had hopes, however, and named their town after the Indian word for silver, Panaca.

Like most Mormon communities, Panaca was a planned develop-ment with blocks and lots of uniform size. The history of the community is likewise peaceful and orderly. During the first four years of the community's life, homes were built, public buildings erected, fields laid out, irrigation systems established and a school founded. The development of mining in the surrounding area and the establishment of the mill town of Bullionville two miles to the west in 1869, however, introduced another historical phase entirely. Mining at Pioche was also getting underway at that time, and other

71

Young members of Panaca's Mormon settlement skating on a reservoir near the community, c. 1908. (Nevada Historical Society.)

such enterprises were either in operation or soon to start at Hiko, Jackrabbit, Bristol and Dry Valley.

The mining communities created a demand for everything produced by Meadow Valley's Mormons—fruit, vegetables, nuts, meat and forage crops—and the farmers and ranchers prospered. This was a mixed blessing and the people of Panaca soon found themselves dealing with unfriendly gentiles, a common Mormon experience and the main reason that they had come west in the first place. The settlers of Panaca also had their troubles with government officials, state and local, since Meadow Valley was included in the 1866 addition to the State of Nevada made by the U.S. Congress. Unlike the settlers of the Muddy, those of Meadow Valley were prosperous enough to pay up and hang on to their farms and ranches. Nevertheless, the proximity of the mining camps remained a continuing problem. Gentile miners would often show up at Mormon dances and other community functions since the mining camps had few women. These men were often drunk, abusive and in a fighting mood as well. Mormons are not generally the type of Christians to "turn the other cheek," and the gentiles were thus a source of much trouble. The mining camps also provided temptations to Panaca's youth—saloons, gambling dens and brothels—which upset both parents and church officials. A good part of the social history of the community revolves around this problem. The Mormons also found themselves on the losing end of decisions over water and land claims in gentile courts, but they stayed to fight it out rather than give in and leave.

Other than the church, the central feature of Panaca's history is the Panaca Cooperative Store, technically the Panaca Branch of the Zion Cooperative Mercantile Institution. Organized in 1869 as a community store, it became the agency for the sale of all grain, flour, foodstuffs and handicrafts produced in Panaca and in central and southern Utah which were destined for marketing in the mining camps of southern Nevada. The co-op also handled all freighting from Utah. Individual church members provided ice, firewood, timber and charcoal to the mines, mills and mining camps and many found employment as miners, millhands and teamsters. The mining camps were also markets for quilts, rugs, clothing and knit goods made by the women of Panaca.

Mining and milling at Pioche and Bullionville peaked in the early

1870s, but the people of Panaca persevered. Markets were developed in the El Dorado Mining District along the Colorado River in southern Utah and northern Arizona, but the people of Meadow Valley were largely self-sufficient needing little from the outside world. In 1892, mining operations opened up at nearby Delamar and another boom era which was to last some fifteen years got underway.

The hardships experienced by the people of Meadow Valley were the same as those of any frontier community, but there was a rich satisfying family life as well. Panaca, the oldest Mormon community in Nevada, remains a quiet, orderly town where the people are proud of their heritage and the achievements of their ancestors.

Bunkerville: Virgin River Mormon Colony

THE VIRGIN RIVER settlement of Bunkerville is the oldest continuously-occupied community, Mormon or non-Mormon, in Clark County. Unlike Panaca and the Mormon colonies of the Muddy Valley, Bunkerville had its origins in the so-called United Order of Enoch, a communal economic scheme propounded by Mormon Church authorities in the 1870s.

The "United Order," as it came to be called, was a reaction to changes occurring within Mormon society in Utah as more non-Mormons took up residence in the territory. Non-Mormons were becoming an increasingly important factor in the economy, and the completion of the transcontinental railroad in 1869 threatened to unleash a flood-tide of gentiles. Mormons found themselves becoming dependent upon outside markets and suppliers for much of what they needed to sustain life. Community co-operatives were common in the 1860s, but Brigham Young and his associates felt that another step had to be taken to extend the principle of cooperation to every phase of Mormon life. The necessity for a new system became even more evident during the economic depression following the panic of 1873 when banks failed, mines shut down, markets in other states dried up and unemployment struck the Mormon heartland.

First set forth by church authorities during the winter of 1873–74, the United Order was based upon the success of a cooperative experiment undertaken by Apostle Lorenzo Snow at Brigham City in 1864 with further refinements as the plan was put into practice. The heart and soul of the plan consisted of the participants' contributing their equipment and properties to the Order in exchange for equivalent shares of capital stock. The members were expected to pledge their "time, labor, energy and ability" and agree to subsist on the products of the Order. A long list of rules were drawn up, and a Board of Management was to be elected to run the institution.

The community of St. George in the southern part of the Territory

Edward Bunker, founder and namesake of Bunkerville in the Virgin River Valley, Clark County. (Nevada Historical Society.)

was the first to be organized under the principles of the United Order and some twenty others followed, but the plan was in trouble from its inception. Disagreements over the use of property and rewards of labor soon surfaced. Those members who considered themselves more industrious resented sharing with the more indolent. There were also resentments over the leadership and troubles stemming from cooperative dining halls and child care facilities where that particular part of the plan was tried.

Approximately half of the Orders dissolved within a year and the parent order, St. George, went under in 1878. One of the failing Orders was established at nearby Santa Clara by Bishop Edward Bunker. Bunker believed that if he could start a new community where there had never been a tradition of private property he could succeed. Obtaining Church approval, Bunker founded a new settlement on the south bank of the Virgin River some thirty miles northeast of the former Muddy Valley colonies.

Arriving with his family, several other relatives and a few friends on January 5, 1877, Bunker established the community which bears his name and set about instituting a system governed by the principles of the United Order as he understood them. Work on a dam and a canal to carry water from the river to a flat selected for cultivation was begun, and the colonists planted thirty-two acres of alfalfa and corn in February. The canal was extended in March and grapevines and vegetables were set out. Fourteen acres of cotton followed in April and sorgum cane was planted in June. A flash flood washed out the dam in August of 1877, but it was rebuilt in time to save the crops.

Labor, duties and material benefits were shared on the principle that all should contribute according to ability and take according to need. There was a common kitchen and dining room for a time, as well as a communal child care arrangement. The women rotated household chores and shared work in the fields with their menfolk, but the communal experiment was abandoned within four years due to the same problems which had come to plague previous United Order communities. Each family was finally given responsibility for a certain tract of land and each ate separately, but the settlers still worked together on common tasks, primarily harnessing the unpredictable Virgin River which would regularly defy all efforts to dam it up. New ditches were a cooperative effort, as were community buildings, new homes and new barns. The settlers of Bunkerville also manufactured cheese as a community endeavor for many years.

In many ways, life for the Virgin River colonists was as difficult as that of those who had settled on the Muddy a decade earlier. Insects got the crops, and the heat was as oppressive as ever. Isolation from outside markets was a problem, since the people found that they could not produce everything they needed for themselves. Malaria was also common at Bunkerville, and the water from the river was so muddy, alkaline and foul that it was virtually undrinkable even when boiled and treated. Those who drank it were often afflicted with an ailment known only to that small section of Nevada, "Virgin Bloat," a peculiar type of indigestion that defies description and is not covered in the medical literature.

Agriculture continued to flourish in Virgin Valley, and relations with non-Mormons improved over the years. County and state officials gave no cause for complaint. The people soon began to think of themselves as Nevadans, not displaced Utahites. The success of the Bunkerville settlers brought other Mormon families to an area just across the river and slightly upstream in 1880. The community of Mesquite was established, but the forces of adversity caused the settlement to be abandoned two years later. Dudley Leavitt later moved over from Bunkerville with his family to re-occupy the site and Mesquite remains Mormon to this day. Settlers also began to move back into the Muddy Valley communities of Overton, St. Thomas and St. Joseph. The last was renamed Logandale, but St. Thomas was abandoned when the rising waters of Lake Mead inundated the community in 1938.

The Mormons of White River Valley

DESPITE THE DECLINE in Mormon immigration from Europe in the 1880s and 1890s, there was still a need for new colonization areas. A combination of factors—Utah's persistently high birthrate and a long agricultural and mining depression in the period 1873 to 1896—forced many Mormons to settle outside the state since there were few arable areas left in Utah. The last of the "Utah Pioneers" thus had to look elsewhere—Wyoming's Big Horn Basin and Star Valley, the Grand Ronde Valley in eastern Oregon, scattered locations in Idaho, Arizona and New Mexico and the White River Valley south of Ely in northeastern Nevada.

Immigrant trails dating back to the 1840s crossed that isolated section of Nevada, and a passing traveler once described the valley as "an ocean of undulating wheat grass standing as high as a horse's belly." Those who first settled the area in the early 1860s were inclined to agree, but it was a rather bizarre set of circumstances which brought the Mormons to the area in the spring of 1898.

Congress passed a law in 1862 banning the Mormon practice of polygamy, plural marriage, but it was never enforced in Utah. Subsequent anti-Mormon legislation in the 1870s and the 1880s was more effective in pressuring church officials, and the Edmunds-Tucker Act of February 19, 1887, provided for the confiscation of all church properties in excess of a total value of $50,000. Church authorities transferred property to private ownership before the law went into effect, but this subterfuge was disallowed by the courts. Among the property taken over by a federal receiver were 30,000 sheep and 75,000 cattle, most of which were farmed out to the White River Valley Land and Livestock Company of White Pine County.

As a consequence of the Edmunds-Tucker Act, church president Wilford Woodruff issued a manifesto on September 25, 1890, proclaiming an end to plural marriages. Other economic and social concessions induced Congress to begin returning church property in 1894. Additional property was returned in 1896, the year Utah was

Panoramic view of White River Valley, the site of Mormon settlements Lund and Preston. (Nevada Historical Society.)

granted statehood. An unforeseen problem with the return of some property was that many no longer existed. The "White Winter" of 1889–1890 killed most of the Mormon sheep and cattle placed in Nevada and a settlement thus had to be arranged. In compensation, the owners of the White River Valley Ranch tendered all their land, livestock, buildings, equipment and other property in White Pine County. Church officials accepted the offer and began making plans to occupy and develop the ranch. By this time, church officials were no longer controlling every aspect of colonization, but rather were forming joint stock companies. The Nevada Land & Livestock Company was set up in 1897 to oversee this new acquisition. The Mormon church provided financial assistance and held a large block of stock, but the company was an ordinary commercial enterprise otherwise.

In March of 1898, the first settlers arrived from Moroni, Utah. Others came a few weeks later and the communities of Preston and Lund were established that summer. Drawings were held for home lots and five- and ten-acre farm plots each with water rights. Lund, named for Apostle Anthon H. Lund, was located on the east side of White River Valley, and Preston, named for Bishop William B. Preston, was established on the west.

The first settlers constructed makeshift shelters shortly after their arrival, but substantial frame and rock homes soon came to grace the communities. A two-story log meetinghouse which also served as a school was erected at Lund in 1900, the same year the first church ward was organized. Preston did not have a similar public building until 1903.

As Mormon enclaves within a largely gentile political entity, the people of White River Valley were left to handle their own affairs. Bishop's Court, presided over by the Bishop and two counselors, handled most disputes between the settlers, and there was also a High Council where decisions could be appealed. The matter of further land sales by the company which would have an effect on limited water supplies was decided by higher church authorities.

A group of Mormons also settled the Steptoe Valley, a 560-acre site where East Ely is now located; and the community of Georgetown was established. In 1902, the land and water rights were sold to the New York and Nevada Copper Company, and the twenty-five families who had located there joined the other settlers at Lund and

Preston. Danish and German converts also began to arrive shortly after the turn of the century and church services in those languages were held for many years.

The subsequent history of the White River Mormons remains to be written. The relationship of the people to their fellow citizens in the county and the state needs to be examined, as does the influence of the mines in the Ely area thirty-five miles to the north. The most we can say at present is that Lund and Preston remain Mormon, as do Panaca, the communities of the Muddy Valley, Bunkerville and Mesquite.

PART FOUR

Famous Nevadans

Richard Jose: Blacksmith Balladeer

AMONG THE FEW Nevadans who have made their mark in the entertainment world was Richard Jose, a Cornish lad who got his start singing in Virginia City's saloons at the tender age of nine.

Born in Lanner, a village in England's Cornwall section on June 5, 1869, young Richard was sent off to an uncle in Virginia City in 1878 following the death of his father. The uncle, Albert Jose, a Cornish miner on the Comstock, had offered to take the boy, but had left Virginia City for Butte, Montana, before his nephew arrived. With only a mailing tag attached to the lapel of his coat and a few coins in his pocket, Richard was left to fend for himself and make his way in the world as best he could.

Too young to enter the mines, he considered taking odd jobs around town, but soon turned to a talent learned at his father's knee, singing. There were some thirty saloons in Virginia City at that time, most of them heavily patronized by Cornish miners, "Cousin Jacks" as they were known. Walking into one of them on his second night in town, he stepped up to the bar and began singing "Where Is My Wandering Boy Tonight?" The miners paused to listen and he followed up with "The Lone Grave," a Civil War ballad which was popular in Cornwall. When young Richard told the miners of his Cornish origins and his circumstances, they pressed money upon him and invited him back.

Jose made the rounds that night and the next, and he was soon sending money home to his poverty-stricken mother and his younger brothers and sisters. The young man's new career brought him to the attention of a group of reform-minded Comstock ladies, however, and they put a stop to it by forbidding barkeepers to allow him in their establishments. He drove a bakery wagon for a time before moving on to Carson City. The state's capital had fewer saloons than Virginia City, but the young balladeer's attempts to entertain the patrons brought the same response as that of the ladies of the

Richard Jose, a Cornishman whose career as an opera singer began in Virginia City. (Nevada Historical Society.)

Comstock—banned. He then moved on to Reno to live with an uncle, William J. Luke, who had a blacksmith shop on the corner of Fourth and Sierra Streets.

Jose became known as Reno's blacksmith balladeer, and many Renoites would stop by Luke's place to hear him sing as he pounded out horseshoes, sharpened tools and repaired wagons and farm equipment. He was called upon to sing at churches and public benefits, and he began to take voice instruction from a teacher at Bishop Whitaker's School for Girls.

In 1884, a friend who had become the manager of a California minstrel troupe introduced him to Charles Reed, a booking agent, and he joined one of Reed's troupes in Sacramento at a salary of $12 a week. The troupe next played in San Francisco, where Jose was soon making $100 a week. As his fame grew, he was offered a position in New York City with the famed Lew Dockstadter's Minstrels at $150 a week. Once on Broadway, Jose was taken to heart by the city's music lovers, and he introduced more songs there than any performer in history. In the 1890s, he began to make annual tours of Europe where he sang for the crowned heads of every nation. On a tour of South Africa, the famed Cecil Rhodes closed down his diamond mines so his employees could hear Jose sing. At Montreal, Canada, the organist stopped in dead silence, awestruck by Jose's voice. During the Spanish-American War, he entertained at troop encampments. Theodore Roosevelt, commander of the Rough Riders, halted a patriotic parade and saluted as Jose gave a rendition of "Good-by, Dolly Gray" from a street platform.

Jose also began to record for the Victor Talking Machine Company and made the company its first million when he cut "Silver Threads Among the Gold," the song which became his signature. When silent movies became popular after the turn of the century, Jose performed in one of the earliest, "Silver Threads Among the Gold," in 1911. For its opening in New York's old Madison Square Garden, Jose stood in the wings watching the movement of his lips on the screen and singing his famous theme song. In a sense, the film was the first "talkie."

When it became apparent that Jose's voice did not adapt well to radio, he gave up singing in the 1920s. In 1919, California Governor William D. Stephens appointed him to the position of Deputy Real

Estate Commissioner, a job he held until his death on October 20, 1941. Although largely forgotten in America by that time, he is still remembered in his native Cornwall. A silver trophy donated in Jose's honor by some American friends is annually awarded to the best musical choir in Cornwall.

Hank and Horace

SOME MEN ARE born to greatness, others achieve it by dint of a lifetime of study and hard work and few achieve it by some fluke of history. Such is the case with Hank Monk, an otherwise obscure stagecoach driver who happened to be in the right place at the right time.

In June of 1859, Horace Greeley, the famous New York editor and social reformer, was touring the area he had so earnestly been recommending to the young men of his section of the country. Tarrying too long in western Utah Territory, Greeley feared that he might miss his scheduled lecture appearance on June 30 in Placerville, just over the Sierra in California. At an inn near Genoa on June 29, he told the keeper of his problem and of his desire to hire a coach and a driver for a quick trip. The man who came forward was Monk, thus securing a memorable place in western history.

The trip began at dawn on June 30 and was one both men would not soon forget. Monk hurtled his coach and his passenger at full speed up and down the narrow grades, over boulders, streams, felled trees and bone-jarring ruts. Horrified at the prospect of ending his days at the bottom of a cavernous ravine, Greeley, at one point, yelled up to Monk, "Driver, I am not particular about an hour or two." Monk then uttered the words which would go down in history, "Keep your seat, Horace. I told you I would get you there by five o'clock and by God I'll do it if the axles hold."

Monk was as good as his word and a frightened, somewhat disheveled Horace Greeley arrived on time for his speech. Because of his prominence, the story spread throughout the country and became a standard item in the repertoires of traveling lecturers. Greeley himself narrated the exciting ride in his own newspaper, the *New York Tribune,* but he later came to regret the whole incident. As embellished by such writers and lecturers as Mark Twain and Artemus Ward, Greeley came off looking like a "timid Eastern greenhorn" and Monk became the "daredevil stage driver." Monk himself told

Hank Monk, famed stagecoach driver whose journey with Horace Greeley carved out a niche in history for them both. (Nevada Historical Society.)

and retold the story thousands of times in exchange for drinks and became the best-known driver in the West.

Greeley could not live the tale down and it haunted his subsequent political career in the 1860s, a version even being read on the floor of the U.S. House of Representatives in March of 1866, much to the amusement of those present. When Greeley ran for President on the Democratic ticket in 1872, it again came up, but he had become such a comic figure on other issues by that time that his defeat was almost a certainty. Monk, still driving stages in the Sierra, wrote to Greeley at that time asking some small favor or government position, but was harshly rebuffed. Denying his request, Greeley wrote "I would rather see you 10,000 fathoms in hell than ever give you a crust of bread, for you are the only man who has had the opportunity to place me in a ridiculous light, and you villainously exercised that opportunity, you damned scamp."

Greeley died shortly after his 1872 defeat, but Monk lived until 1883 when he died of pneumonia. Every editor in the West noted his passing and one suggested that Horace should be on hand at the pearly gates when Hank arrived, a blazing chariot and a team of angels under his rein to send him spinning over the golden pavements at a speed which would remind him of other days.

Albert A. Michelson: Nevada Nobel Laureate

AMONG THE MANY Nevadans who have made their mark on the world was Albert Abraham Michelson, America's first Nobel Prize winner in physics and the only American since Benjamin Franklin to be awarded the Copley Medal of the Royal Society of London.

Born on December 19, 1852, at Strelno, a small Prussian village near the Polish frontier, Michelson came to America with his family in 1854. After a short stay in New York, the family moved to San Francisco. Michelson attended schools at Murphy's Camp in Calaveras County. In 1867, the Michelson family moved to Virginia City where his father, Samuel Michelson, established a dry goods store.

Samuel Michelson had educational aspirations for his son, and the boy took the examination for a Congressional appointment to the U.S. Naval Academy at Annapolis. Tied with another young man, Michelson lost the appointment through political influence exerted on behalf of his competitor. Undaunted, he got a letter of recommendation from Congressman Thomas Fitch and set off for Washington, D.C. to try to get one of the ten appointments at large from President Grant. He talked with Grant but the appointments had already been made. Going on to the Academy, he so impressed the Commandant with his earnestness that a place was made for him at the school as an eleventh appointment.

At the Academy, Michelson developed an interest in music, art and athletics. His proficiency in math and science was remarkable. He accrued more than the average number of demerits, but graduated ninth in a class of twenty-nine on May 31, 1873. Following two years of naval service in the West Indies, he was appointed an instructor in physics and chemistry at the Academy where he taught until 1879. That year he was assigned to the Nautical Almanac Office in Washington, D.C. under Professor Simon Newcomb who was undertaking studies of the measurement of the velocity of light. Michelson became his assistant, but left the naval service a

Albert A. Michelson of Carson City, winner of the 1907 Nobel Peace Prize in Physics. (Nevada Historical Society.)

year later to study in Germany and France. In 1883, he became a professor of physics at the Case School of Applied Sciences. He moved on to Clark University in 1889 and to the University of Chicago in 1892.

Michelson had meanwhile been continuing his experiments on measuring the velocity of light, and his work helped to establish the astronomical yardstick used to calculate universal space, the speed of light. He also conducted experiments on ether drift with Dr. Edward W. Morley and took up the study of optical interference. In regard to the latter, he also made contributions to the fundamental apparatus and theory in spectroscopy. In 1900, his echelon spectroscope was one of the earliest to have sufficiently high resolution to disclose optical evidence of molecular motion which is identified with temperature, and his interferometer defined the international standard meter in terms of wavelengths of light. Michelson's Nobel Prize was awarded for his work in spectroscopic and meteorological investigations. His work with light was later to become part of a new philosophy of science which reached its highest development in Albert Einstein's theory of relativity.

Michelson continued his interest in naval affairs. In Chicago he organized and commanded the Illinois Naval Militia. Of the six patents he was granted, five were for optical range finders he designed for the Bureau of Ordnance between 1891 and 1919. During World War I, he was a lieutenant commander working on rangefinders and solving the very practical problem of what imperfections in American substitutes for German optical glass could be tolerated in binoculars.

As a teacher, his lectures were considered models of organization and clarity of exposition, and his intuitions with respect to natural phenomena were unprecedented. He was also a talented violinist and had remarkable skills in oils and watercolors. At an exhibition of some of his watercolors, an art patron once told him that he had made a great mistake when he abandoned art for science. He replied that he had never abandoned art since it was his conviction that in science alone was art able to find its highest expression.

In May of 1948, the U.S. Navy dedicated a large new laboratory to Michelson at the ordnance station at China Lake, California. In later years this laboratory was expanded to embrace the whole research complex. On exhibit is an impressive array of Michelson's instruments, publications, records and other memorabilia, but the man himself was more complex than anything he left behind. A fellow scientist, writing after Michelson's death in 1931, characterized him as pursuing "his modest serene way along the frontiers of science, entering new pathways and ascending to unattained heights as leisurely and as easily as though he were taking an evening stroll."

George Washington Gale Ferris

WITH THE EXCEPTION of the square-set timbering system developed by Philipp Deidesheimer which is still in use in mining operations around the world, there are very few technological innovations attributed to Nevada engineers. One of the very few operating today is the Ferris Wheel, which was invented by George Washington Gale Ferris, a famous engineer who spent his boyhood in Carson Valley and Carson City.

Born in Galesburg, Illinois, in 1859, Ferris moved to Carson City with his family in 1863 after a short residence in nearby Carson Valley. He received his early education in Carson City and later was enrolled in a military academy in Oakland, California. Following his graduation, he entered Rensselaer Polytechnic Institute in Troy, New York, where he received his engineering degree in 1881.

Taking up railroad work, he was employed in a contracting office in New York City for a time, but soon moved on to a position with the Baltimore, Cincinnati & Western Railroad in pushing a rail line across West Virginia. In 1882 he became an engineer with the Queen City Coal Mining Company in West Virginia. In this position, he was responsible for building a large coal trestle on the Kanawha River and three 1,800-foot tunnels.

Interested in bridge building, Ferris secured positions with several bridge companies and achieved some note for his work with concrete under heavy pressure in pneumatic caissons. In 1885, he was placed in charge of testing and inspection of iron and steel work for the Kentucky and Indiana Bridge Company of Louisville. Foreseeing an increase in the use of structural steel, he familiarized himself with the process involved in the manufacture and developed a new profession. In 1887, he organized the firm of G. W. Ferris & Co. at Pittsburgh to conduct mill and shopwork inspections and testing throughout the country. After the business began to function smoothly, he turned his attention to the promotion and financing of large engineering projects and was involved in the construction of

George Washington Gale Ferris, inventor of the Ferris Wheel. (Nevada Historical Society.)

The Ferris Wheel at the World's Columbian Exposition in Chicago, 1893. (Nevada Historical Society.)

bridges across the Ohio River at Pittsburgh, Cincinnati and Wheeling, West Virginia.

When Daniel H. Burnman, chief of construction for the World's Columbian Exposition scheduled to be held in Chicago in 1893, challenged the engineers of America to produce something to rival the Eiffel Tower of the Paris Exposition, Ferris's imagination was fired. Thinking back to his boyhood days, he remembered the large overshot waterwheels which he once saw along the Carson River and he used the waterwheel idea in designing the Ferris Wheel.

Against the advice of friends and business associates, he undertook the construction of the huge machine, but experienced some money problems in the midst of the severe financial depression which hit the country in 1892. Many engineers looked upon the Ferris Wheel as a fantastic scheme, but Ferris persevered and completed his project shortly after the Exposition opened. Rising more than 250 feet above the Midway and carrying thirty-six gondolas of forty passengers each, it revolved perfectly and was absolutely stable in the strong winds blowing off nearby Lake Michigan.

The daring and accuracy involved in the design and the precision of the machine work won the admiration of Ferris's fellow engineers, and the Ferris Wheel became the most spectacular and profitable feature of the Exposition. Although Ferris's invention was patented and he began to receive royalty checks in September of 1893, he did not recoup the $390,000 the company had expended. In November of 1896, George Washington Gale Ferris contracted typhoid fever and died in Pittsburgh on November 22.

Among those who survived Ferris were three married sisters still living in Carson City, Mrs. A. M. Ardery, Mrs. H. F. Dangberg and Mrs. Charles Schulz. His father had been a well-known horticulturist in Carson City and had planted many of the community's trees. The Ferris home at 311 W. Third Street had become something of a community feature and still stands today. The original Ferris Wheel was not so fortunate. It was dismantled and stored away after the Chicago Exposition and was not reassembled until the St. Louis World's Fair in 1904. The wheel was again taken apart after the fair and later sold for scrap, a sad loss to those with a love for the technological history of America.

Edna Purviance: From Lovelock to Hollywood

AMONG THE FEW Nevadans to carve out a niche in the history of the movies is Edna Purviance, a Lovelock girl who became Charlie Chaplin's leading lady in 1915 and starred with him in thirty-five films during the Silent Era. The daughter of Mathew and Louise Davey Purviance, she was born in Paradise Valley, a small ranching community in northern Humboldt County, on October 21, 1896. After the death of her father, her mother married Robert Nurnberger of Lovelock. Nurnberger also passed away when Edna was a girl and her mother kept the family together by running a boardinghouse.

Edna was a striking beauty from her early girlhood and seemed destined for bigger things in life than Lovelock could offer. She not only had talent as an artist, but was an accomplished pianist as well. During her high school years she also appeared in several dramatic productions.

Following her graduation, she went to San Francisco to live with an older sister who worked as a diving belle at the Panama–Pacific International Exposition. She took a business course at a local college and secured employment as a typist, but she spent her evenings at Tate's Cafe on Hill Street, a haven for the city's artsy crowd. Among those with whom she struck up an acquaintance was Carl Strauss, a handsome German-American who had already broken into the movies in Hollywood as a cowboy. Strauss had worked with G. M. "Bronco Billy" Anderson of the Essanay Film Company which had recently put Charlie Chaplin under contract. The budding comedian needed a leading lady to fill out the stock company, and he and Anderson went to San Francisco in 1914 to look over the chorus girls in one of the film producer's musical comedies playing there. The girls were shapely and beautiful and Chaplin enjoyed the talent search, but none was photogenic. Strauss then told Chaplin of Edna and introduced the two. The little comedian had mixed feelings about the Nevada girl. In his autobiography, he later characterized her as "more than pretty, she was beautiful," but seemed "sad and

Edna Purviance, a Lovelock native who made it big in Hollywood as Charlie Chaplin's leading lady. (Nevada Historical Society.)

serious" at the interview. "She was quiet and reserved, with large beautiful eyes, beautiful teeth and a sensitive mouth. I doubted whether she could act or had any humor, she looked so serious. Nevertheless, with these reservations, we engaged her. She would at least be decorative in my comedies."

Edna's success in Chaplin's films was not happenstance or fortunate accident, as it would seem. Indeed, Chaplin knew what he was doing when he selected her. Like Mack Sennet, he appreciated the value of having beautiful girls in the comedy format because of the strong undercurrent of sex upon which it thrived. Chaplin also preferred leading ladies whose performances he could mold rather than those whose screen style was already formed, those who reflected his own ideal image of womanhood rather than being performers in their own right. Edna seemed perfect for everything Chaplin had in mind for the future. Blond and classically statuesque, she was the perfect foil for his dark coloring and temperamental humor. She was also unpretentious, calm and agreeable—never ruffled by Chaplin's often bizarre antics in the early years.

Edna and Charlie fell in love almost immediately, and she took an apartment near the Hollywood Athletic Club where he lived. Their relationship was to endure for many years, and she remained with Charlie's company as an actress and with Charlie as his mistress, even though he married Mildred Harris in 1918. After his divorce in 1920, their relationship was much the same as before, although Edna increasingly found herself surrounded by handsome admirers. She also knew how to make Charlie jealous and the press played up scenes, fights and dramatic reconciliations between the two.

Edna's film career had all but come to an end by 1924 and she and Charlie were emotionally estranged, but they were still close enough to encourage press speculations. When Lita Grey, Charlie's second wife, filed for a divorce in 1926, Edna was named in the petition as one of several correspondents. As to why Edna and Charlie never married, the little actor is vague. In his autobiography, he wrote as follows: "We were serious about each other, and at the back of my mind I had an idea that someday we might marry, but I had reservations about Edna. I was uncertain of her, and for that matter uncertain of myself."

As an actress, Edna's performances served only to highlight Charlie's comic genius, and she never developed an acting career independent of her work with him. Indeed, of all the actresses he launched, only the latter ones, Paulette Goddard, whom he married in 1936, Dawn Addams and Clair Bloom, became stars in their own right. By 1923, Edna had become "rather matronly" in Charlie's view, no longer suited to the comedy format. He also felt that she had developed as an actress and deserved a role in more serious films. The result was *A Woman of Paris* in 1924, written and directed by Charlie himself. Adolph Menjou played the male lead and Charlie appeared only briefly in the film. Although the picture flopped at the box office, it served to launch Menjou's career. However, it also marked Edna's departure from the silver screen.

Chaplin never forgot Edna. To the day of her death, January 13, 1958, in Cedars of Lebanon Hospital in Los Angeles, he kept her on his company's payroll at a salary of $1,000 a month. In Nevada, Edna has been all but forgotten, those who once crowded into the theatres to see her pictures having died or moved on. There are no monuments to her in Pershing County, no streets or buildings which bear her name, no record of her school days in Lovelock. Only the ladies of the Humboldt County Museum in Winnemucca remember her. At the museum, they have one of her flapper-style, beaded dresses on exhibit. The dress, worn in the 1917 film *The Adventurer*, was once blue, but is now a faded grey. The museum also has a scrapbook of clippings relating to Edna's career which is available to those interested in the life of this unique Nevada girl.

Cyrenius B. McClellan

KNOWN TO HIS friends as "C. B.," or simply "Mac," C. B. McClellan was perhaps Nevada's best-known artist of the 19th century. Born in Pennsylvania in 1827, he arrived in California in the mid-1850s. In San Francisco, he worked in the studio of a prominent still-life artist, but little is known of his training otherwise. He later had studios at Marysville, Forest City, Downieville and other California communities, but his only known surviving works are those he completed in Nevada.

McClellan came to Virginia City and set up a studio at 9 North C Street in 1868. In addition to taking portrait commissions from those Virginians wealthy enough to have themselves immortalized on canvas, he painted signs for merchants and saloonkeepers and did mural renderings for the decoration of saloon interiors—tigers, jungle scenes, even the Arabian desert on one occasion. He also did landscapes—a panorama of Gold Hill, for example, showing all the hoisting works and mills, and another of the Morgan Mill on the Carson River with the Mexican Mill and the community of Empire in the distance. A panoramic masterpiece of the country lying east of Virginia City got no further than the sketching stage. Seven years of work on it was destroyed in the big fire of October 26, 1875.

As McClellan's fame spread, he became more diverse. In 1876, during the trial of John D. Lee, he painted the scene of the infamous Mountain Meadows Massacre. He also once rendered a scene from the Civil War—a duel with swords between a Confederate officer and a Union officer. The background was complete with red glare, smoke, wrecked gun carriages and fragments of caissons strewn about.

McClellan's most famous painting was completed in 1882, a panorama of Myron Lake's toll bridge across the Truckee River and the original Lake House surrounded by sagebrush and boulders. Entitled "Reno Twenty Years Ago," it was apparently done in two versions, one with only the inn and the bridge, and a second showing Myron

Lake's Crossing in 1862 as depicted by artist Cyrenius B. McClellan. (Nevada Historical Society.)

Lake himself, Chief Winnemucca and several other Indians standing in the foreground. One of these was sold at auction in 1883 and carried off to California and it is not known if it ever returned. Copies of the paintings abound, however.

In addition to capturing the wealthy on canvas, McClellan did much work on speculation in hopes that someone would buy. So enthused was he with his art that he often painted for nothing or did work for his friends who were too poor to pay. He once did a portrait of the French writer Victor Hugo, but refused to sell it to John Mackay since he had promised it to a friend. As it happened, McClellan was in one of his financially destitute periods at that time and hardly knew from where his next meal was coming.

At various times, McClellan had studios in Virginia City, Gold Hill, Carson City and Reno, but he never became wealthy. When he was in the chips, however, he was the toast of the town. "Open-handed and generous," a newsman once wrote of him, "he cast his earnings about among all who chose to partake of his hospitality, which never knew any limit so long as he had money in his pocket."

The loss of his Virginia City studio in the fire of 1875 not only destroyed much of his work, but burned up his brushes, easels, paints, mixing pans and other equipment. As the mines of the Comstock fell upon depression years in the early 1880s, McClellan's commissions became fewer and farther between. With no family to look after him and his friends of former days unwilling to help, he passed his final years in Reno working on studies of Nevada Indians and trying to get up a subscription to enable him to paint a picture of the late President Garfield. Although he was only in his early fifties by that time, his health broke down. Those who knew him claimed that he did not eat right or otherwise take care of himself, but his well-known fondness for the bottle was also a factor in his break-down. On the morning of October 1, 1883, he was found dead in his Reno hotel room. He was laid away at Reno's Hillside Cemetery two days later.

Francois Pioche: Forgotten Nevada Financier

LIKE THE COMSTOCK LODE, the mining areas of southeastern Nevada were developed by outside capital. As a rule, those who invested did so on speculation and few of them ever saw the mines and mills they financed or ever visited the mining camps which developed. One such man was Francois Louis Alfred Pioche, a San Francisco banker and financier who contributed his name to the present-day county seat of Lincoln County.

Born in France in 1818, he studied law and worked in the French Ministry of Finance as a young man. After squandering an inheritance from an uncle, he was able to get a Foreign Service appointment in the French Consular Office in Santiago, Chile. He left the position to join J. B. Bayerque in a mercantile business and began to make his fortune. When word of the discovery of gold in California reached Chile, Pioche and Bayerque left Santiago for San Francisco with a cargo of merchandise. Arriving in February of 1849, they opened a general merchandise store on Clay Street and began to specialize in French imported goods. As time passed, they became bankers, first storing the miners' gold in their safe and later lending out their excess capital.

In 1851, Pioche returned to Paris to seek funds for more extensive financial ventures. He also promoted San Francisco through the issuance of a series of engraved views of his beloved city. The firm of Pioche & Bayerque acquired extensive real estate holdings in what is today San Francisco's Financial District and in the then undeveloped Mission District. Pioche also financed the Market Street railway, one of the city's earliest transit systems, and bought extensive tracts of land in several counties in the 1850s and 1860s when the old Spanish and Mexican land grants were being broken up and sold.

Pioche was among a group of businessmen who financed the Johnson Street Wharf Company, one of the first private wharves to extend into the bay, and was a member of a business organization

Francois Louis Alfred Pioche, mining entrepreneur after whom the
town of Pioche is named. (Nevada Historical Society.)

which unsuccessfully sought to obtain the shore area of the bay for private use. Other financial ventures included the San Francisco Gas Works, the principal component of what is today Pacific Gas & Electric, and the Spring Valley Water Company which is today part of San Francisco's municipally owned water system.

The enterprising Frenchman imported chefs from France, and San Francisco soon had numerous restaurants with excellent reputations for fine French cuisine. One of these was Le Poule D'Or which Pioche backed personally. Americans soon corrupted the name and it is today The Poodle Dog. Pioche backed industrial fairs in his adopted city, contributed to charitable and philanthropic causes and promoted cultural and educational enterprises. He was also a bon vivant and collected works of art, fine furniture and rare books.

Pioche's mining enterprises included the Temescal tin mines in southern California, the Malakoff diggings at North Bloomfield, California, the New Almaden Quicksilver Mine near San Jose and various hydraulic mining operations. In Nevada, he was involved with the Twin Rivers properties near Belmont in 1868 and mines in the Ely Mining District whose principal community, Pioche, bears his name. In 1869, he incorporated several properties as the Meadow Valley Mining Company. This company became one of the largest operations in the district and constructed the first working smelter in the area.

Pioche, whose name was adopted for the new camp laid out in the Ely Mining District in January of 1869, never visited his Nevada holdings and took no part in the operation of the Meadow Valley Company. At a miners' meeting held on March 11, a letter from S. E. C. Williamson was read in which Pioche's name was suggested. A rich lode in the district already bore his name, and those at the meeting accepted the suggestion to christen the town after him.

The Meadow Valley Company operated until forced to close when the mines bottomed out in the summer of 1876, but Francois Pioche did not live to see the end of his enterprise. On May 2, 1872, he placed the muzzle of a heavy Navy Colt revolver to his head and committed suicide. The reasons for the taking of his own life are not known. Some friends said that France's defeat in the Franco-Prussian War in 1870 had unnerved him, but others cited his guilt feelings for his role in the San Francisco Vigilance Committee lynchings in the 1850s. He also suffered from severe headaches as a result of a fall from a horse, and there is a possibility that business reverses known only to himself and a few associates led to the deed. In any case, his only legacy is a short street near Bernal Heights in San Francisco, a plaque on the site of his first banking house on Clay Street and the Nevada mining camp named in his honor. He deserves better.

PART FIVE

Nevada's Mines and Miners

Andrew S. Hallidie

AMONG THE TECHNOLOGICAL innovations spurred by Nevada's Comstock Lode was the development of flat wire cable for hoisting ore buckets and mine cages. Prior to the opening of the Comstock in the 1860s hemp and manila rope served well enough, but Nevada's mines were of such depth that rope could not be made sufficiently strong to support thousands of feet of its own weight together with a loaded ore bucket or cage. The unequal bending of the strands broke them and damp rot burrowed insidiously within. Chain was not perceptibly better since the links would not run smoothly and lie properly on the hoist drum. When kinked, one link would often break the weld of the adjacent link. Frapping parallel iron wires into a bundle by a continuous fiber wrapping was also tried, but the wires kinked, broke and deteriorated even faster than the materials they replaced.

True wire rope was invented by John Augustus Roebling, who later designed and began the construction of the famed Brooklyn Bridge. It came into use in the 1850s when galvanization and oil coating were developed to prevent internal corrosion and kink breakage. Soon, however, it was replaced in western mines by the braided, flat wire cable invented by Andrew S. Hallidie, an English immigrant. Born in London in 1836, Hallidie went to California in 1853. When his dreams of wealth in the gold fields came to naught within two years, he took up surveying and flume construction. His father had been involved in the manufacture of wire rope, and the young man adapted some of his early training to build a wire suspension structure for a flume over the American River. The span was 220 feet across, and Hallidie constructed another fourteen of the structures in the United States and Canada over the next twelve years.

In 1857 Hallidie got into the business of manufacturing wire rope in San Francisco, founding A. S. Hallidie & Co. in North Beach. This company later became the California Wire Works. In connection

Andrew Smith Hallidie, inventor of the flat wire cable pioneered on Nevada's Comstock Lode and the father of San Francisco's cable car system. (Nevada Historical Society.)

with this enterprise he developed the flat wire cable. Three inches wide and one-half an inch thick, a 1,300-foot length would weigh only 1,297 pounds. First installed in a mine at Gold Hill operated by the Croesus Gold & Silver Mining Company in the spring of 1864, the cable proved vastly superior to round wire rope. It would wind flat on the barrel of the windlass, was less likely to slip and provided better control when lowering buckets or cages loaded with miners. So successful was the innovation that it was universally adopted on the Comstock, and its use spread to mining operations the world over.

Ever the innovator, Hallidie went on to invent and perfect a method of transporting freight over canyons and rough surfaces by means of endless wire ropes which became known as the "Hallidie Ropeway." The success of the ropeway suggested the application of the same principle to the pulling of loaded streetcars up the steep hillsides of San Francisco, work then performed by horses. By 1871 he had developed an endless underground cable and a mechanical gripping device to be attached to the underside of streetcars. Ridiculed at first by the public and considered a visionary by those with money to invest, he persisted and completed an installation on Clay Street in August of 1873. The system was so successful that it was soon installed on other streets and was adopted by other cities as well.

Andrew Hallidie was a Regent of the University of California, President of the Mechanics Institute of San Francisco and Vice-President of the James Lick School of Mechanical Arts. He was also a founder of the San Francisco Public Library and Art Society, a member of the committee which framed San Francisco's municipal government charter and a member of the Executive Committee for the World's Columbian Exposition held in Chicago in 1893. Hallidie died in his beloved San Francisco on April 24, 1900, with the famed cable car system his only public memorial. However, a station on the Bay Area Rapid Transit System, a monumental transportation project, was named in his honor in the 1970s.

Gone but not forgotten, another of the many immigrant boys who contributed to the development of California as well as Nevada.

Philipp Deidesheimer:
Pioneer Engineering Genius

AMONG THE MANY ironies of history is the fact that the Comstock Lode would not have developed into the most famous silver mining district in the United States without the work of an obscure German mining engineer, Philipp Deidesheimer.

Born in Germany in 1832, Deidesheimer enrolled at the Königliche Sächsische Bergakademie at Freiburg in the silver-rich province of Saxony. At that time, the Freiburg school was to mining what the Sorbonne in Paris was to arts and letters. Among the important mining men who came out of the school were the famous geologist Baron Von Richthofen and pioneer Nevada metalurgist Charles A. Stetefeldt.

Deidesheimer migrated to the American West in 1851 seeking opportunity, fame and wealth. Arriving in San Francisco by ship, he began working on the placer diggings in El Dorado County, California. When the placers proved to be less rich than he had anticipated, the young engineer started lode mining operations of his own, achieving local fame for his technological innovations.

The opening of silver mining on the Comstock Lode in 1859 posed mining problems which had never been faced before, chief of which was the extreme depth and breadth of the ore bodies. In the Ophir Mine, to take but one example, the ore body at 180 feet was found to be 45 feet wide. Since the surrounding ground tended to shift and the ore bodies were also soft, the lives of the miners were in constant danger from cave-ins.

Mining operations on the Comstock had almost come to a halt by the summer of 1860. William F. Babcock, a San Francisco agent for the Pacific Steamship Company and a Trustee of the Ophir Mining Company, contacted Deidesheimer at his mine in Georgetown, California and arranged to have him brought to Virginia City to look into the problem of timbering the deep mines.

One characteristic shared by all mining engineers is the ability to initiate and adapt, but Deidesheimer's first weeks in Nevada were

116

Philipp Deidesheimer, pictured with his wife, is the famed mining engineer who is remembered in history as the inventor of square-set timbering. (Nevada Historical Society.)

frustrating. Descending again and again into the bowels of the Ophir Mine, he would return exhausted. Finally the inspiration came. According to Louise Rinkel, daughter of Deidesheimer's friend, Mathias Rinkel, the engineer came out of the mine one day and threw himself in the sagebrush. As he lay there, he watched some bees gathering honey. Following them back to their hive he watched the worker bees building combs, and the idea of building the famous square set timbering system came to him in a flash. Deidesheimer and Rinkel drew out the design that night and three days later hewn timbers for the first sets were lowered down the Ophir Mine.

The system worked so well that it was soon adopted by other Comstock operations and its use spread to mining the world over. Had he patented the system, millions of dollars in royalties would have come Deidesheimer's way. As he once told Matt Rinkel, "If all goes well and these square sets protect the lives of the miners, what more could a man ask for?"

Deidesheimer's only reward was a permanent position as the Ophir Company's superintendent and a chance to get in on some good mining prospects. He did well through his investments in the Ophir properties and others, but lost it all in stock market speculation and the bottoming out of the Comstock Lode in the early 1880s.

Deidesheimer worked on Ophir properties in Montana for a time and completed an engineering survey for bringing water from Lake Tahoe to San Francisco. By the turn of the century, he was in San Francisco dealing in real estate, but was wiped out by the earthquake and fire of 1906. In 1912, he was reported to be in poor health and destitute financial straits. Four years later, July 21, 1916, he was found dead in a cheap hotel in San Francisco.

Nevada editors reported on his death, but only C. C. Goodwin, an old-time Nevada newsman, added a personal note. Writing in *Goodwin's Weekly* from Salt Lake City, he commented as follows: "We suspect that sometimes his dreams were disturbed by hunger, old fashioned plebian hunger. If they were, we are sorry, for could he have his way, no living creature would have been hungry. And now the merciful earth has opened her arms and taken him to rest, shading his eyes from the light. May his sleep be sweet."

Union War at Treasure Hill

THE LOT OF WORKING men in early-day Nevada was a hard one. With the exception of the Comstock Lode, unions were weak and wages and working conditions were largely determined by capital and management. If a man were injured on the job, he had no recourse other than an expensive lawsuit against his employer or the hope that the company would take pity on him and his family. If he were killed in an accident, his fellows would help his widow for a time, but she would eventually be thrown upon her own resources. When wages were cut, there were usually divisions in the ranks as to what course of action to take, and the union was soon out of favor with the public if a strike closed down a mining operation.

Some of the earliest unions in the West were on Nevada's Comstock Lode, but one of the most violent early labor disputes took place in the camp of Treasure Hill in White Pine County during the summer of 1869. At that time, the mines were paying good wages of $5.00 a day for ten hours labor and there were few complaints. On July 11, officials of the Eberhardt Company announced that wages were to be reduced to $4.00 effective the following Monday. This move caused consternation throughout the district, and even the editor of the local newspaper, a pillar of the establishment, protested.

Management representatives claimed that the ore from the mines was becoming progressively less rich, but rumor had it that the wage reduction was part of an attempt to "bear" the stocks of all Treasure Hill's mines so as to enable San Francisco speculators to pick up some bargains.

Other stories circulated to the effect that the operators of the Eberhardt and other mines wanted to reduce wages to the point that white miners would leave the district and cheap or Chinese labor could be hired. When officers of the White Pine Miners Union called a strike, 740 men agreed to walk out. Many miners remained on the job, however, and on July 14 a mob of striking men visited several

119

The Eberhardt Mill and surrounding mines, Treasure Hill, Nevada
scene of a heated labor dispute during the summer of 1869. (Nevada
Historical Society.)

mines and exacted promises from superintendents to keep wages at the old level. Higher management overruled the superintendents, which brought on planning for another march. Management then threatened to shut down and lock the remaining miners out.

Internal disputes were beginning to break out in the union ranks, but a second march was held on July 27 and four-dollar men everywhere were forced to quit work. Teamsters were also prevented from loading, and storekeepers in Treasure Hill retaliated by cutting off all credit to union men. The issues were becoming increasingly confused and in early August a "Four-Dollar League" was formed by those men whose families were getting desperate. A "Five-Dollar League" was then organized and mine operators began to exploit both sides.

At 3:00 A.M. on August 3, twenty disgruntled miners, all members of the "Five-Dollar League," raided three Treasure Hill mines and drove off the men working the night shift with clubs and pistols. At the Hidden Treasure shaft, rocks were thrown down upon the working miners, who were assaulted with clubs when they came to the surface. Others were fired upon and one fleeing man fell into a fifteen-foot open pit and broke his leg. Similar incidents also took place at the Summit and Nevada Mines.

Shortly after dawn, news of the previous night's work circulated and threats of lynching were bandied about. Cooler heads prevailed and the sheriff from nearby Hamilton arrested six of the leaders of the mob. Others who had taken part either caught an early stage for Elko or otherwise laid low.

As might be expected, the incidents worked to the disadvantage of the more peacefully inclined strikers and the union. Membership rolls and records were seized as the community turned against the union men. Additional arrests were made and union officials soon disbanded their organization, although they had neither known of the raids beforehand nor approved of them. In subsequent trials, each man was fined $25 and court costs.

Mine owners hailed their victory which lowered ore reduction costs from $35 a ton to $20. These reduced costs induced more outside capital to invest in the mines and eventually more mine and mill men were hired than had been working before, but workers did not get a second opportunity to organize. The Treasure Hill District remained nonunion until its mines played out in the mid-1870s.

The Deadly Dust of Delamar

IN MINING OPERATIONS throughout the world, human life has been a part of the toll exacted for the supply of metals and minerals which keep our industries going. Nowhere was this more true than at the camp of Delamar in southern Lincoln County which became the widow-maker of all time.

The initial discoveries at Delamar were made in 1889 by John Ferguson and Joseph Sharp, two local ranchers engaged in trapping wild mustangs in the Highland Range bordering Meadow Valley Wash. Both filed several claims in Pioche, the county seat, and they were soon selling shares in their enterprise to raise money for development. The grubstakers sold their rights to others interested in the area, Ferguson and Sharp eventually realizing some $10,000 for their efforts.

The man who wound up with the best claims was Joseph Raphael De Lamar, a native of the Netherlands who had had a varied career as a sea captain, a slave trader, a salvager of sunken ships, a member of the Idaho Legislature and a promoter of mines in Colorado and Idaho before he ventured into the business in Nevada.

In May of 1894, shortly after De Lamar took over, the community of Helene was abandoned, and the inhabitants moved down to an open flat just south of the major mining area. The new community took the name Delamar, running the promoter's name together as a single unit without the extra capital letter.

A fifty-ton chlorination mill was soon under construction, and milling and smelting began in February of 1895. Over the next five years, some $9,000,000 in gold was produced, but Delamar became better known for the deadly dust which killed or permanently disabled hundreds of miners and mill hands. Although the mines were worked to a depth of 1,000 feet, very little moisture was encountered. As a consequence, the ore was very dry and would crumble easily. At times, the dust problem made conditions almost unbearable, but it was in the mill where it did its most deadly work. Most

122

The mining camp of Delamar, Nevada, known far and wide as a
widow-maker. (Nevada Historical Society.)

mill workers lasted only five or six months before falling ill. The dust settled in the lungs, piercing the tissue like ground glass and bringing on an ailment that was more like quick consumption in its symptoms than any other disease. Most men wore respirators, but to little avail, as the tiny particles got into the lungs just the same. Indeed, those who did not wear the protective devices lasted about as long as those who did.

Company officials refused to recognize the dust as the source of the "fever," as it was sometimes called, but technological change eventually eased the problem. In 1899, a Kansas City Dust Collector was put on the market and one was installed at the mill. An additional attractive feature of the device was the fact that it also saved tiny particles of gold which had been passing into the atmosphere. Since the collector thus paid for itself, the company installed a whole battery of them.

When dust in the mines continued to be a problem, the company began an investigation. Under the microscope, the particles appeared to be quartz grains with sharp points and edges. Once in the lungs, the bits of quartz would irritate and weaken the tissues until a hemorrhage was started. Miners and mill hands were not the only victims. Delamar fever also affected women and children in the community. The mill was located uphill from the residential area, and the dust thus blew over the town much of the time. Because the men also brought it home on their clothing, the deadly crystals soon permeated everything.

The exact number of victims is not known, but physicians familiar with the camp later claimed that 500 deaths would be a very conservative figure. This writer's estimate, based upon different types of calculations, would be 1,000 and up since many men and their families who had lived at Delamar had their lives shortened by some years, even though they may not have known the origin of the final ailment which killed them. Others were sick and debilitated and their subsequent lives were not as happy and productive as they might have been.

Journalists made much of the problems of the camp, and one cold-blooded writer figured that the deadly dust of Delamar cost the life of one man for every $15,000 that Captain De Lamar made in profits. In any case, De Lamar died a wealthy man in December of

1918. He had not forgotten the Delamar experience when he made his will, however. Half of his $20,000,000 fortune was left to the medical schools of Columbia, Harvard and Johns Hopkins universities with the stipulation that the funds be used for research on the origins of human disease.

General Grant's Visit to the Comstock

As the centerpiece of the great Comstock Lode, Virginia City was known far and wide. No visit to Nevada was considered complete without a tour of the mines. Among those of some note who made the excursion were former President Ulysses S. Grant and his family in October of 1879.

Word of the coming of the famous Civil War hero and political leader had spread some months before, and Virginia City was a mass of flags, shields, streamers and wreaths when the Grant party reached the Comstock on the 27th. People from the surrounding towns began to flock in that morning, as did the local Paiutes and even the usually quiet Chinese were seen to be dodging everywhere to get a look at the big "Melican war man."

At 11:00 that morning, Virginia City's militia companies, the firemen and state, county and city officials marched in a body down the Divide to the Gold Hill Depot where the visitors were to debark from the train. A great crowd had collected in and about the depot. A few minutes before 1:00, the appointed hour, the scream of steam whistles could be heard coming from American Flat. The boom and bang of anvils and giant powder cartridges soon blended with the music from the bands, and shouts of "Here he comes" arose as the train chugged up the grade.

A detachment of militiamen cleared a portion of the depot platform, where Grant, his wife and Governor John Kinkead stepped out to a welcome by the Mayor of Virginia City. Following the Mayor's address, the parade over the Divide to Virginia City began as artillerymen posted on the Bullion Dump fired a twenty-one gun salute. When the parade reached the crest, the children decked out in their "bibs and tuckers" waved small flags and cheered in their small, shrill voices. The procession wound through the streets and ended at the Savage Mine Office, where Grant was to review the remainder of the procession and speak from the east balcony.

Mrs. Grant had arrived in Virginia City on the V & T Railroad and

The Grant party at the mines in Virginia City, October 28, 1879. (Nevada Historical Society.)

was conveyed to the Savage office in a six-horse carriage. Following her arrival, Senator John P. Jones, Senator William Sharon and several members of the Reception Committee gathered on the balcony. Grant's speech was short and to the point, thanking the people for their hospitality and claiming he was not like Nevada's Senators ". . . who are in the habit of making long speeches and catching your votes." Sharon and Jones spoke briefly, as did James G. Fair. At 3:00 P.M., a reception was held for the veterans of the Mexican War and the Civil War, both Union and Confederate, and the militia companies went through their maneuvers. The fire companies performed that day in addition to the local Paiutes.

A reception for Grant and his party was held at the Storey County Courthouse that evening. Above the entrance was a large painting showing the General in full uniform shaking hands with a miner. Beneath the painting was inscribed, "The Miner's Welcome to the Soldier." All who desired to call upon him that evening were welcomed, and the party repaired to Piper's Opera House about an hour later. Grant's entrance into his box was the signal for the entire audience to stand and applaud. The General bowed, took his seat and seemed to enjoy the play. Dinner was served at the Savage Mansion later that evening.

In honor of the famous visitor, the people of Como, some twenty miles to the southeast, built an immense bonfire on their tallest peak. As the sun went down the people of Virginia City witnessed a rare and beautiful phenomenon. The American flag waving from the top of Mt. Davidson picked up the rays of the setting sun and appeared as if it were wrapped in flames. This same thing had happened once before during the Civil War on the occasion of the Union victory at Appomattox Court House, and it was taken as a good omen.

The next morning, the party was escorted to the C & C Shaft where they were joined by Governor Kinkead, John Mackay, James G. Fair and others for a trip to the lower levels of the Consolidated Virginia and California Mines. All changed to the grey woolen shirt and pants of the miner with heavy shoes and coarse felt hat to match. They first descended to the 1,750 foot level where Mrs. Grant expressed herself as being agreeably disappointed at finding all so light, dry and comfortable. She expected the lower levels to be dark, wet and muddy. Mrs. Grant and the other ladies returned to the surface at that point, and Mackay conducted the men down to the 2,150 level where the temperature reached 120 degrees. Although it seemed a bit warm for the others, Grant did not appear to mind and asked many questions about the timbering, the running of the shafts and other work in progress there.

Back on the surface a few minutes later, the group was assembled for Johnny Noe's camera. At 4:00 that afternoon, a reception was held at the Pacific Coast Pioneer's Hall, where Grant was made an Honorary Member. After thanking those who had accorded him the honor, he remained for the musical program and to view the cabinets of relics and curiosities in the hall. That night, the General and his party once again visited Piper's Opera House and enjoyed a performance by the Colville Company.

Next morning, the distinguished visitors went down to Sutro and took breakfast at the Sutro Mansion. They then traversed the Sutro Tunnel up to the Savage Mine and came to the surface in Virginia City. At 1:00 that afternoon, Grant and his wife said their farewells and were off for Carson City and Reno and on east to Washington D.C., fully confident that all was well with the mining industry and that America was on a firm industrial footing.

Hardrock Miners

THE TRADITIONAL IMAGE of the miner in the American West is that of a prospector with a pan and shovel accompanied by his faithful burro. However, to understand the hardrock miner is to understand industrial mining in the West as opposed to the placer miner in the gold fields of California.

The hardrock miner in Nevada needed strong physical endurance to work the deep mines since it was necessary to swing an eight-pound hammer in cramped quarters and manage a drill accurately in poor lighting. The miner had to be able to judge the number of shots which would be required to bring down an ore body, where to put the holes and how deep to drill them for maximum effectiveness. He had to be able to recognize waste rock, gauge the strength of the surrounding walls to determine the type of timbering needed and had to know enough surveying to keep the workings lined up.

Miners usually worked an eight to ten hour shift for a wage of $3.00 to $5.00 a day. Whatever romantic notions one might hold about hardrock mining would quickly be dispelled by a visit to the mines and a short talk with the men on shift. The heat in the lower levels of the Comstock, for example, was often 150°F or more. The miners usually wore only a light breech-cloth and thicksoled shoes to protect their feet from the scorching rocks and steaming rills of water that trickled over the floors of the drifts. Each man voraciously consumed ice and ice water, periodically dunking his head under a shower of water flowing from conduit pipes, and paused frequently to fill his lungs with fresh air at the open ends of blower tubes.

Heat exhaustion took its toll on the hardrock miners, as did their emerging half-clothed and sweating from the steaming depths of the mines into the chill mountain air of the Comstock. The shock often sent them home half choked with pneumonia and spitting blood, but finally led to the establishment of change rooms where the men could shower and put on dry clothing before braving the elements. Differences in air pressure above and below ground caused many

A crew going on shift at the Ophir Mine, Virginia City, 1898.
(Nevada Historical Society.)

miners to get the "bends" when taken up too quickly. The heat and the ice water also had a strange effect upon the miners' appetites and caused a craving for such highly seasoned foods as pickles, salads, pig's feet and ham—almost anything with an acid or salty flavor.

In addition to heat, the hardrock miners also suffered from foul air because of inadequate ventilation. The stench from human excrement, rotting timbering, carbonated ground waters and gasses from the materials used in blasting nauseated them. There was a constant danger from carbon dioxide accumulation causing a loss of consciousness and suffocation; lesser concentrations caused headaches, weakness and dizziness.

The most deadly affliction of the miners was silicosis, a disease caused by the breathing of fine silica and quartz dust from drilling and blasting. In the nineteenth century the disease was not understood, and it was blamed on such factors as the dark, dank atmosphere of the mines or the poisonous gasses from nitroglycerine. The only real solution to the problem was wet drilling and effective ventilation, alternatives that came long after many men passed their final years in the clutches of lung disease.

Accidents in the mines were almost an everyday occurrence. Some can be attributed to the fact that there were no standards for mine excavations and no safety inspection programs, but others came as a result of overconfidence, absentmindedness or sheer carelessness. Accidents in the cage hoisting the men out of the mines came from dizziness due to the extreme change in temperatures, but careless operation of the hoist by the engineers and falling tools, timber or rock also took their toll. Some men simply walked off the edge of the main shaft and were torn apart as they bounced off the walls while others were scalded to death when they fell into the sumps at the bottom. Blasting accidents, ("missed holes" in the parlance of the miners) caused injury and death, as did the caving in of the overhead rock when seams swelled from exposure to air or inadequate timbering.

Hardrock miners were not the only men to face the rigors and dangers of life underground. Muckers used to load the ore cars, carmen to run the ore out, timbermen to brace up the ore bodies, engineers and mechanics to operate and maintain equipment, blacksmiths to reforge dull drills and picks and messengers to carry tools, orders, water and ice to those laboring underground were all part of the mining operation.

High-Grading and Highgraders

MINING COLLEGES and textbooks on mining engineering in the nineteenth century prepared students for most everything they might find in the field, but the practice of high-grading—the pocketing of extremely rich gold ore by miners working in the depths of the mines—was seldom mentioned. From the miners' point of view it was merely a perquisite of the job, but to the mine owners it was outright theft. All miners denied doing it and all of them were accused, but the best that the owners and superintendents could do was to keep the practice to an irreducible minimum. Men who were joint owners and worked their own mines would not pilfer from themselves, however, mining companies owned by distant, anonymous stockholders were constantly victimized.

Since mineralization in a gold lode is seldom of uniform distribution, miners might blast and muck for weeks without seeing any hint of metal at all. Then, without warning, they might suddenly come across an extremely rich natural concentration of gold nuggets the size of marbles. Any man would be tempted by such a find.

The lunch pail was undoubtedly the first and favorite method of getting high-grade out of the mine at the end of a shift, bandy-leggedness sometimes being ascribed to certain miners because of the great weight of their lunch receptacles. Specimen bosses hired to examine pails at quitting time, however, put an end to this practice. Nevertheless, mine owners gained little from inspections, as the miners simply devised other means of concealment. Some acquired a capsule-like tube of baked clay which could be concealed in the rectum and was thus undetectable, although a miner might be stripped for searching. A more thorough search by the specimen boss foiled this ruse, as did the practice of having the suspect miner squat down and lift a heavy set of bar bells.

Small smears of clay covering nuggets were sometimes placed about the body, but a shower or a dip in a vat of water washed them off. A variety of other means were also devised—a double or false-

133

B 2485. Raiding of a High Grader's Cache. Goldfield. Nevada

Raiding the office of a bogus assayer, Goldfield, 1907. Assayers were a critical link in the crime of high-grading valuable ore. (Nevada Historical Society.)

Members of a Goldfield mine crew, c. 1907. (Nevada Historical Society.)

crowned hat which could hold up to five pounds of rich ore, a long sock or cloth tube suspended inside a trouser leg, small pockets sewn inside a waistband of the trousers or false cuffs. The miners also devised an apparatus known as a corset cover, a chemise-like affair worn beneath the shirt and likewise equipped with pockets. Excessive greed might well subject a man to a double hernia, but the risk was cheerfully accepted.

Some mining companies eventually set up change rooms where the miners going off shift could discard or store their soggy work garments, shower under the eye of a supervisor and put on street clothing. The highgraders often circumvented the change room by enlisting the supervisor and offering him a share of the proceeds. In the Nevada camp of Goldfield the change room practice became an issue in a bitter labor dispute. Discovering that they were losing up to forty percent of their bullion through high-grading, officials of the Goldfield Consolidated Mining Company established change rooms. Urged on by the leaders of the Western Federation of Miners and the radical Industrial Workers of the World, the miners struck and threatened to take over the town and all the mines. President Theodore Roosevelt finally dispatched three companies from the Twenty-Second Infantry Regiment from San Francisco in December of 1907, and the strike collapsed.

Since the people of most mining camps encouraged high-grading, slugs of melted-down ore and dust were accepted without question in saloons, brothels and honky-tonks. Prosecuting attorneys had a hard time convicting highgraders because the average juror had good reason to suppose that he himself might be in the dock the next time around. Even the clergy dealt gingerly with the practice. A mining company in Goldfield once paid a preacher to excoriate the sin of theft during a Sunday sermon and he did right well until he came to high-grading. Gauging the temper of his congregation, he concluded his oration by remarking, "but gold belongs to him what finds it first," a novel, but welcome exegesis of the Eighth Commandment.

PART SIX

Roughnecks, Robbers and Outlaws

Silent Jim's Manhattan Saloon Scam

Jimmy Hicks, prospector, poet and inveterate gambler, created a sensation wherever he went. To the people of the mining camp of Manhattan, "Silent Jim," the monicker his friends gave him, was the man who pulled off the most ingenious scam in history.

Hicks drifted into Manhattan in the fall of 1906 and acquired a nearby mining claim. The few dollars he grubbed out of the ground inevitably found their way to the men behind the tables. On December 17, 1906, Jim entered the Bank Saloon, walked to a corner and set down his bag of provisions and a case of dynamite. As he stepped to the bar for a drink, the dealers livened up the atmosphere. "Shoot six, Jimmy Hicks, that's the line," hollered a craps dealer. "It's a cat hop, two-for-one for a call," said the lookout in the easy chair of the faro game. The stud poker dealer announced that chips were a dollar a stack and that a chair was waiting for a good player. Stud was Jim's favorite game and he took a seat.

As always, Jim was stripped of his last cent within the hour. Dejected, he rose from the game after politely refusing the offer of a drink as consolation. A look of pity shadowed his handsome face, a look that seemed to say "I pity myself for my own weakness." He walked to the corner, picked up his bag and the case of dynamite and shuffled toward the door. Reaching the stove, he paused, turned to the miners at the bar and said, "Boys, I am weighed down tonight with sorrow. I feel I must relieve myself of a portion of the burden." He then offered to tell them something of his past, and the men gathered around. He told them of how he had left a happy home in the East to seek his fortune out west and of how he could have made it if he had not taken up gambling. "That's what makes me blue tonight," he said. "The money I lost would have taken me on a visit to those nearest and dearest to me." He began to read a letter he had received from his mother that day, but burst into pitiful sobs after a few lines. "Excuse me boys," he said, "but I could not restrain the tears. When I look back and see the kind old face of mother as she

Booming Manhattan, Nevada, 1906. (Nevada Historical Society.)

kissed me good bye with God's blessings for her son on her lips, it almost drives me mad." Swearing off gambling forever, he stooped and picked up the box of dynamite. Gazing into the eyes of his fellows, he said, "And upon my word, it is the last game any of you men shall ever play." He then thrust aside the stove lid and threw the box into the flames.

The scene which followed beggars description. Every man made a mad dash for the door as tables and chairs were smashed aside. Three men crashed through the front window, and two others ran out the rear exit, battering down the door in their haste. A good half-mile was covered by the terror-stricken little band before they stopped for a breath, but no explosion was heard.

After a lengthy wait in the snowstorm they returned to the saloon. The bartender slowly opened the door and went inside. The room was just as he had left it, but an examination of the till behind the bar revealed that it had been stolen as well as the money on the tables. On the mirror behind the bar, the following note was found: "The box was empty boys. I'm off to lift the mortgage from the old home and marry Mame. I'll remember you when blowing in the coin."

The World's Last Stage Robbery

ROBBING STAGECOACHES was not as profitable nor as frequent as Hollywood writers would have us believe; however, the practice has become an enduring part of the mythology of the West. Surely nobody knows the exact number of stages robbed by enterprising Westerners, but it is recorded in the annals of history that the last robbery took place on December 5, 1916, at Jarbidge, an isolated gold camp in northern Elko County.

Every saloon in town was packed that snowy evening as the miners went about their nightly rounds of drinking, gambling and wenching. The fact that the stage from Rogerson, Idaho, was three hours late was commented upon by several men who were expecting mail, but the condition of the road from the north due to the weather was thought to be sufficient reason for such a delay.

About 7:00 P.M. the town's postmaster, Scott Fleming, asked Frank Leonard to ride to the top of Crippen Grade to see if he could sight the stage. Leonard returned an hour later having seen nothing. This development caused some concern that the stage had slipped off the grade and plunged into the river, but all present knew the driver, Frank Searcy, was a veteran with a four-horse team, having negotiated the narrow shelf of a road many times.

When the stage did not show up for another hour, plans were made to investigate the cause of the delay. While these preparations were underway, a Mrs. Dexter from the north end of town ambled into the Success Bar and told the men that the stage had passed her house about suppertime. "I'm positively sure of it," she said. "The driver was huddled on the seat as if he were terribly cold and had his coat collar turned up around his face. I called to him and asked if he wasn't about frozen, but he didn't answer."

The post office was only a half-mile south of Mrs. Dexter's place and yet the coach had been missing for three hours along that short stretch of road. The miners quickly realized that something was amiss which had nothing to do with the weather, so they formed a

Ben Kuhl, convicted of stagecoach robbery and murder in Jarbidge, Nevada. (Nevada Historical Society.)

search party. Within a half-hour the missing coach was located in a clump of willows a couple of hundred yards off the main street with Frank Searcy slumped over the seat inside with a bullet hole in the back of his head. The horses were tethered in their traces to a nearby tree, and the second-class mail sack lay in the snow, its contents scattered over the frozen ground. The first-class pouch containing some $4,000 in gold coins was missing.

Darkness prevented further investigation, and armed guards were posted to prevent anyone from leaving town. The next morning it was determined that the killer had swung aboard the empty coach as it descended Crippen Grade, some distance north of Mrs. Dexter's residence. Searcy had apparently been shot right away and the horses, startled by the blast, ran with the stage for a hundred yards or so before the murderer was able to get them under control.

Bloodstains in the road indicated that it was the murderer who was at the reins when the stage passed Mrs. Dexter's, a fact which accounted for the driver not showing his face or responding to her greeting. Shortly thereafter, the driver had turned the coach off into the thicket, tethered the horses and set about robbing the mail pouches.

Footprints of a large man and paw prints of a dog were found leading from the stage to the river. The tracks went through the willows to a path that crossed a footbridge over the river and entered the business section of Jarbidge. As the miners tramped up and down the road in search of clues they were joined by an old dog, a type found in every mining camp, owned by no one but everybody's friend. At one point after the dog joined them, the animal suddenly bounded off into the willows and began pawing at the snow. The hound soon uncovered the first-class mail pouch with blood-smeared letters inside, but not the package containing the gold coins. Someone quickly matched the dog's paws with those found near the footprints and concluded that the animal had indeed followed the murderer.

It was known that a local miner, Ben Kuhl, had been particularly fond of the dog, allowing the animal to live in his cabin. There was additional evidence that linked Kuhl to the crime. Searchers found a bloody shirt and coat tucked beneath the bridge. They were of the type commonly worn by miners, but Kuhl's partner, Edward Beck, recognized the coat as one which had hung in their cabin for some time and was available to anyone who happened to walk in and take it off the hook. Also found in the cabin was a .45 caliber revolver in a suitcase lying upon a freshly laundered shirt with a bloodstain beneath it. The weapon had recently been fired and one chamber was empty. Kuhl denied ownership of the gun, and it was later determined that it belonged to a friend of his who had borrowed it from someone else who had originally borrowed it from a saloonkeeper to shoot rats in his cabin. All those involved in the borrowing and loaning of the weapon were arrested, but only Kuhl was unable to account for his whereabouts on the night in question.

The trial was held in Elko in September and October of 1917 where a web of circumstantial evidence was wound around Kuhl. In addition, prosecuting attorneys introduced a new line of evidence: a letter from the mail pouch smeared with a bloody palm print. Fingerprint experts convinced the jury that the print matched that of Kuhl rather than any other suspect. Kuhl maintained his innocence while his attorney, Edmund E. Caine, fought heroically, taking advantage of every technical point for later appeal to higher courts. Caine struggled against desperate odds, and on October 6, 1917, the jury returned a verdict of murder in the first degree. Kuhl was sentenced to be shot on January 10, 1918, but an appeal to the Nevada Supreme Court for a new trial caused a stay of execution to be issued.

As the appeal was being considered, Kuhl confessed to the murder of Searcy. He claimed that the robbery was a frame-up arranged between himself and Searcy and that they had planned to split the money. Kuhl said that Searcy did not keep his end of the bargain and had tried to kill him, thus forcing him (Kuhl) to act in self-defense. When asked about the money from the holdup, Kuhl claimed that a friend had taken part of it to pay for attorney Caine's services and had left town with the remainder.

Kuhl's confession earned him a commutation of his death sentence, but he was turned down for parole twenty-seven times before being released in the spring of 1955. Over the years, the story has spread that the $4,000 in gold double eagles is still buried somewhere in the vicinity of Jarbidge where treasure hunters periodically try to uncover the money from the last stage robbery.

The Lynching of Joe Simpson

WILLIAM "NEVADA RED" WOOD of Hazen was the last victim of a lynch mob in Nevada; however, he was not the last Nevadan to "stretch rope." That honor goes to Joe Simpson, a former Reno cook and restaurant owner who was lynched in Skidoo, California, on April 22, 1908.

Simpson had an unsavory reputation in Reno where he once had the roof of his mouth and part of his nose shot away during a dispute over a poker game. After going broke in the restaurant business in Reno, he migrated to Fallon before going south to the boom camps of central Nevada where he ran restaurants in Gold Reef and Rhyolite. The fall of 1907, Simpson went to Keeler, California, where he reportedly murdered a man who had cheated him in a card game. Somehow he got off, but decided that another climate would be more conducive to his health, hence, his move to Skidoo on the eastern edge of Death Valley.

At the California camp, he became the partner of Fred Oakes in the Gold Seal Saloon. On April 19, 1908, he was wandering the streets drunk, threatening the lives of peaceful citizens going to and from church. A few men, tiring of such behavior, took him in hand and bound him to a telegraph pole until he sobered up. He was drunk again that afternoon when he staggered into the Skidoo Trading Company and asked manager Jim Arnold what he had against him. Upon being told that Arnold had nothing against him, Simpson pulled a revolver and said, "Prepare to die; I am going to kill you," whereupon he fired, inflicting the wound that killed the storekeeper a few hours later.

Simpson was arrested within minutes and locked in a cabin belonging to the local deputy sheriff, which served the town as a jail. A preliminary hearing was set for April 23, but as the time approached, feelings against Simpson hardened. A decision was made to save the county the expense of a trial.

On the evening of April 22, a posse of masked men surrounded the

146

Joe Simpson and his wife standing to the rear at a restaurant they operated in a central Nevada mining camp before he became the victim of a lynch mob in 1908. (Nevada Historical Society.)

cabin housing Simpson and demanded he be surrendered to them. Deputy Henry Sellers could do nothing to dissuade the angry miners, and Simpson seemed too frightened to resist. Soon the miners were marching him through the streets in silence while the townspeople hid in their homes and observed the procession. Simpson was marched to the same telegraph pole where he had been tied a few days earlier. Struggling and cursing while the noose was slipped around his neck, he was soon dispatched to the hereafter.

The next morning the usual inquest was held where it was decided that Simpson had "come to his death by strangulation by parties unknown." No further investigations were conducted, and Simpson was buried in a prospect hole on the outskirts of town. "Murderer Lynched with General Approval," read the headline of the local paper on April 23, but it was several days before California editors sent reporters and photographers to cover the story. The citizens of Skidoo were not ashamed of their actions, however, and obligingly exhumed Simpson and hanged him again for the benefit of the cameramen.

There are at least two versions of what became of Simpson's body. According to one version, the body was taken by some prostitutes from Beatty who attempted to carry it across the desert for a proper burial. Somewhere south of Bullfrog, their wagon broke down and they ran out of water, so it was necessary to discard the corpse. Another story is that Simpson was a former patient of a Dr. McDonald who wanted to do research on his skull. Assisted by George Cook, Dr. McDonald cut off Simpson's head. The skull later ended up at Wild Horse Station on the road to Death Valley and was displayed in a showcase for many years. The ultimate fate of the gruesome relic is unknown, but George Cook, many years later, said that it had been discarded in the sagebrush.

George Cook participated in the lynching of Joe Simpson, but never felt good about it. The late Myrtle Myles told this writer that Cook revealed to her that Simpson died of a heart attack before he was strung up. This may be the case, but it might also be an old man's way of salving his conscience over a deed he later came to regret.

The Verdi Train Robbery

THE DRIVING OF THE   Golden Spike at Promontory, Utah, on May 10, 1869, signaled the completion of the first transcontinental railroad, and the beginning of a new era in the history of the American West. The railroad opened up the West to new settlement, created new communities and opened new markets for cattle, timber and other western products. It also provided opportunities for some enterprising Westerners to branch out from bank holdups and stage robbery to train robbery.

The first train robbery on the Pacific Slope took place just west of Reno near what is today the River Inn. The afternoon of November 4, 1870, Central Pacific No. 1 left Oakland, California, for Ogden, Utah carrying $41,800 in $20 gold pieces and $8,800 in silver bars, the coin a payroll shipment for the Comstock mines and the bullion for deposit in Nevada banks to cover commercial drafts.

Meanwhile, five men were holed up in an abandoned mine tunnel on the south face of Peavine Mountain overlooking the Central Pacific right-of-way. A. J. "Jack" Davis, the leader of the gang, received a wire sent by John E. Chapman to R. A. "Sol" Jones that read, "Send me sixty dollars and charge to my account." Signed "J. Enrique." The cryptic message indicated to Davis and his confederates that an express car carrying $60,000 had just left Oakland and would be across the Sierra within a few hours. Davis then began to put the second part of his plan into operation. He and his men rode out at sunset for the old stone quarry near Lawton's Springs where they proceeded to build a tie and rock barrier across the tracks.

The Number 1 was due in Verdi four miles west, about 10:00 P.M. Engineer Henry S. Small was delayed by an accident further up the line, thus it was midnight when he saw the lights of the small lumber town. As the train slowed going through town, five men wearing linen dusters and black masks swung aboard, three onto the open platform of the express car behind the tender and two on the

149

A GROUP OF NEVADA WORTHIES.

Principals in the Verdi Train Robbery. (Nevada Historical Society.)

Jack Davis.   John Squeers.

Jack Davis and John Squires, leaders of the gang that pulled off the Verdi Train Robbery. (Nevada Historical Society.)

back of the car where it was coupled to the day coaches and the night sleepers. Two of the men crawled over the wood pile, dropped down into the engine compartments and covered Small and his fireman with their revolvers. Small was ordered to proceed a half mile east and then whistle "down breaks," long enough to allow the two men on the rear of the express to pull the coupling pin and set the rest of the train adrift. Small was then ordered to proceed to the barricade near the quarry.

Davis took charge and marched the frightened engineer back to the express car and had him knock on the door. "Who's there?" came the reply from guard Frank Mitchell. "Small," the engineer said, whereupon Mitchell opened the door to find himself confronted by three double-barreled shotguns. The men secured crowbars and opened the treasure boxes, throwing the sacks of coin out the side door. Thanking Mitchell for not giving them any trouble, Davis added that they were glad that they did not have to kill him. Davis locked Small, Mitchell and the fireman in the express car while the others stuffed the money into their saddle bags. Mounting their horses, they rode off into the night.

News of the robbery was telegraphed to the Wells Fargo agent in Virginia City, who notified Sheriff Charlie Pegg in Washoe City. Pegg and his deputy, James H. Kinkead, formed a posse of fourteen men and headed for the Sierra, having been informed that the robbers had gone southwest. They found no trace of them in that direction. Unofficial posses seeking the $40,000 in reward money offered by Wells Fargo, the Central Pacific Railroad and the State of Nevada, found evidence that the men had gone northwest toward California.

Jack Davis and his men split the money at the quarry near Lawton's before going their separate ways. James Gilchrist, a miner who was having his first fling as a train robber, E. B. Parsons and John Squires went to Sardine Valley where they took rooms at Pearson's Hotel. Parsons and Squires left the following morning, but Gilchrist remained. When Deputy Kinkead arrived later in the day, he was informed that two men had left for the north, but Gilchrist was still in his room. Gilchrist's actions aroused the lawman's suspicions and he was arrested. Gilchrist identified the other two men and Parsons and Squires were soon arrested. Kinkead wired Nevada Governor Henry Blasdel for extradition papers, and the three were brought back to Nevada. Davis had meanwhile been arrested in Virginia City, and Tilton Cockerell and Sol Jones were found in Reno. Chat Roberts, who ran a stage station at Antelope just across the California line, was also arrested, as was Chapman, the contact man in California.

Sol Jones pleaded guilty and received a five year sentence. Davis got ten years, Cockerell was sentenced to twenty-two years, and both Parsons and Squires received twenty years each. Chapman was sentenced to eighteen years for his part, although he claimed he was in California when the robbery took place.

All but $3,000 of the money was recovered, and there is speculation to this day that it remains buried on Peavine or somewhere along the Truckee River near the site of the robbery. If found, the 150 coins would be worth over $500,000.

Nevada's Last Lynching

FORTY MILES EAST of Reno lies the community of Hazen, a railroad siding which developed in the early part of the twentieth century as a headquarters for construction activity on the canals of the Newlands Project. The town attracted a number of rough characters who kept things lively for the otherwise peaceful-minded citizens. Canal laborers at Hazen were often assaulted and robbed in the streets and alleys, but Churchill County officials assigned only Judd Allen, a local hotel-keeper, to maintain peace.

Typical of the ruffians who gravitated to Hazen was William "Nevada Red" Wood, an ex-convict who had served time at Sing Sing Prison in New York and the Iowa State Penitentiary. Wood previously had been associated with Jerry McCarthy in the operation of a saloon at Derby, another canal camp west of Wadsworth. When McCarthy died under mysterious circumstances in November of 1904, Wood left Derby for Reno. In January of 1905, he was arrested for trying to rob a man outside a Commercial Row saloon, but was released when his intended victim refused to testify against him.

In February, Wood came to Hazen where he and a companion attempted to waylay and rob two canal laborers near the railroad depot. However, the station agent and his telegraph operator intervened. Wood's confederate escaped, but Wood was captured when the telegrapher fired a shotgun over his head. The would-be robber was turned over to Constable Allen, who placed him in the temporary wooden jail which served the town. There was much excitement and some discussion of lynching, but Allen restored calm to the scene and delegated a young stablehand, J. L. Simmons, to keep an eye on things. Allen went back to his hotel about midnight and young Simmons retired to the stable about an hour later.

About 2:00 A.M., a mob assembled and marched over to the jail, smashed the door open with an ax, and ordered Wood to come out. "For God's sake, no," he pleaded, "I'm innocent, spare my life."

The body of William "Nevada Red" Wood, the victim of a lynching in Hazen, Nevada, as caught by the camera, March 1, 1905. (Nevada Historical Society.)

"Come out of there, damn it," came a voice from the mob. Wood was pulled from his cell and dragged to a telegraph pole thirty feet away where a rope was thrown up over the crossbar and a noose placed around his neck. Standing beneath the improvised gallows, surrounded by the mob, he was asked if he had any last words. "Nothing," he said, "only I'm not guilty, for God's . . ." but the rope began to tighten and he was swung into eternity. The end of the rope was tied at the base of the pole and the mob melted into the darkness without further ado.

Wood's body was not discovered until the next morning, when a woman having breakfast at Allen's hotel noticed it but thought it was a dummy. Constable Allen had the body cut down and ordered an inquest. With Justice of the Peace Claud Anderson presiding, they met in a barbershop, considered the telegraph pole and the rope and decided that Wood came to his end by being hanged to a telegraph pole with a rope around his neck.

Allen ordered an immediate burial and a rough casket was nailed together from some packing crates. The casket containing the body was then taken about a mile from town and buried. With the five men who dug the grave on hand as impromptu mourners, Allen said a few words over the casket before it was lowered into the ground and covered.

Hazen's citizens refused to talk to newsmen from Reno, and Sheriff Robert Shirley of Fallon declined to become involved. Governor John Sparks said that he preferred to leave the matter to county officials, although newsmen suggested a number of avenues of investigation. One Reno writer saw the lynching in a larger context, noting that Wood was hanged for stealing a few dollars, whereas the Standard Oil Company and the beef trust stole millions, yet remained unmolested. "A sad state of affairs," he concluded.

One enterprising young Hazenite did a brisk business cutting up the rope used to hang Wood, selling the pieces for souvenirs. A newsman commented that there were enough pieces of rope floating around to lynch all the men who ever disturbed the peace in a dozen such towns as Hazen.

A few days later, Assemblyman James G. Cushing of Nye County introduced a resolution in Carson City condemning the lynching as "a murder of the first degree and a disgrace to the state and the civilization of the age." R. Leslie Smaill, Churchill County Assemblyman, saw to the defeat of the measure, however. "We believe that lynching should be condemned," he said, "yet we do not believe that the people of Hazen should be censured for an act that any community would be guilty of. I voted against the censure and I will do so again."

The lynching of "Nevada Red" Wood was the last ever in Nevada, bringing to an end a tradition which had begun in 1858 with the lynching of "Lucky Bill" Thorrington in Carson Valley. It was long past the time for it.

PART SEVEN

Prize Fighting in Nevada

Blood, Sweat and Leather:
The Baer-Uzcudun Fight

ALTHOUGH RENO is best known as a center for gambling and the "divorce trade," the city has achieved a niche in history as the scene of several significant boxing matches. Marvin Hart and Jack Root fought there on July 3, 1905, for the honor of succeeding retired heavyweight champion Jim Jeffries, who, on July 4, 1910, attempted a comeback against Jack Johnson. The third fight for which Reno is noted was a brutal twenty-round brawl between Max Baer and Paolino Uzcudun which took place on July 4, 1931.

The Baer-Uzcudun fight was promoted by Jack Dempsey, the famed ex-heavyweight champion who had arrived in Reno in April of that year to seek a divorce from his actress wife, Estelle Taylor. Dempsey had been refereeing and promoting fights since he failed to regain his title from Gene Tunney in the controversial "long count" decision on September 22, 1927. Some two weeks after his arrival, he lined up James McKay and William Graham as backers for a fight. Charitably described by the press as "sportsmen," Graham and McKay were associates of financier George Wingfield, and were perhaps the central figures in the illegal drug, liquor and prostitution activities that Reno was noted for at that time.

Several leading heavyweight contenders were considered for the match, but the decision finally came down to Baer, a dashing Livermore, California, heavyweight whose career had suffered some recent setbacks, and Uzcudun, a Spanish Basque who had been a leading candidate to succeed Gene Tunney until his defeat by Max Schmeling in 1929. To build interest in the fight, Dempsey promised the winner a crack at Jack Sharkey, the number one contender for Schmeling's crown. He also talked of making a comeback himself and of promoting Reno as the center for boxing nationally. Minor disputes among various managers, trainers, and sparring partners were magnified in the press, and the upcoming fight began to take on all the trappings of a major contest. Among those who arrived for the fight were luminaries of the boxing world, sports

Paolino Uzcudun, Basque heavyweight pugilist who fought Max Baer in Reno on July 4, 1931. This photo was taken at Steamboat Springs, the site of Uzcudun's training camp. (Nevada Historical Society.)

writers of national fame whose experiences with Nevada boxing went back to 1897, and all the odd, assorted characters who seem to gravitate to "happenings" of any sort.

Uzcudun trained at Steamboat Springs where hundreds of his Basque countrymen observed his sessions, while Baer, training at Lawton's Springs (today's River Inn), drew equally large crowds. A number of rising fighters were drawn to Reno to serve as sparring partners, and Reno fight fans were treated to fight cards almost nightly at an arena on Chestnut Street (today's Arlington Avenue) operated by Reno promoter Frankie Neal. Dempsey himself was often present for the fights and sometimes acted as referee or took off his coat to give the fighters a few pointers.

Ticket offices were set up in several major western cities, and city officials in Reno soon became aware that they might have an influx of 20,000 or more fans on their hands. Entire trains were reserved out of San Francisco, Los Angeles, Salt Lake City and Seattle; thousands of other fans were driving or flying in. Hotels were booked solid in advance, auto courts were jammed, and makeshift "tent cities" were spread around until city health officials feared an outbreak of typhoid fever due to crowded conditions and inadequate sanitary facilities. Also concerned was the Reno Chief of Police who secured two Thompson sub-machine guns to help deal with any expected trouble. The gambling houses hired special armed security guards, and Reno citizens were beginning to wonder what they had let themselves in for.

McKay and Graham financed the construction of a new clubhouse and arena at the state fairgrounds, and had made extensive improvements on the horseracing track. The day of the fight was a scorcher, and several Renoites who were among the 15,000 spectators told this writer that the heat boiled the pitch out of the fresh pine boards in the grandstand and ruined their pants. Under the merciless sun, Baer and Uzcudun went at it for a solid hour—twenty bruising rounds!

Uzcudun's fighting style was crude but effective, consisting mainly of rushing his opponent and taking any amount of punishment to get inside and land a few heavy blows. Baer had a classier style and knew something of the science of boxing, but the fight was a brawl from the opening bell. Both men were bloodied by the fifth round, and sweat was soon running the dye in their trunks and turning their legs purple. Baer threw several rabbit punches, and both men butted heads and wrestled each other around the ring. Each missed several opportunities to put the fight away, but by the end of the fight Uzcudun had worn Baer to the point that he was almost on his last legs. The decision could not have gone any other way and Dempsey, the referee and sole judge, raised Uzcudun's hand in victory.

Ironically, Baer's stock in the fight game rose after his defeat, while that of Uzcudun declined. After beating several tough opponents, Baer defeated Primo Carnera on June 14, 1934, to take the heavyweight championship which he held about a year before being defeated by Jim Braddock. He later had a brief movie and radio career and died in Hollywood in 1959. Uzcudun fell upon hard times and retired to his native Spain after being knocked out by Joe Louis on December 13, 1935. He later became a supporter of Generalissimo Francisco Franco in the Spanish Civil War and was wounded during the conflict. In later years, he was the Chief of Police of the city of Valencia and became quite wealthy investing in real estate.

As to Jack Dempsey, he received his divorce in September of 1931, in the midst of a comeback which he had begun in Reno shortly after the Baer-Uzcudun Fight. On September 7, he fought three men at the fairgrounds in an exhibition before leaving Reno for mining ventures in the Gold Circle District of Elko County, and a comeback tour through the Pacific Northwest and the Mid-West. His comeback fizzled with his defeat by King Levinsky in Chicago in March of 1932, and he was back in Reno in April to promote a second fight, a bout between Baer and Levinsky.

The clubhouse and grandstand erected for the Baer-Uzcudun Fight was later taken over by the State of Nevada and served as offices and quarters for livestock shows and rodeos. During World War II, an aviation training school was located there and the building was partially destroyed by fire. In 1950, the Washoe County Agricultural Extension Service moved into the structure. Another fire in June of 1962 destroyed the grandstands and damaged the building, but it remains the headquarters of the Extension Service and is still referred to as the "Dempsey Building" by old-timers and those who work for the agency.

Jack Dempsey

THE WORLD KNEW HIM AS Jack Dempsey, Heavyweight Champion of the World, 1919–1926, but he was Kid Blacke before that and William Harrison Dempsey before that. Now that the great champion has taken the final count, it might be appropriate to sum up the Nevada phase of his life.

Born in Colorado in 1895, he grew to manhood on a ranch near Provo, Utah, where he spent his leisure hours punching bags of sand and sawdust and dreaming of a boxing career such as his elder brother, Bernard, was pursuing. His first fights saw him pitted against nobodies in nowhere towns in Colorado and Utah, but he had bigger aspirations.

Arriving in Reno in April of 1915, he took what work he could find to keep body and soul together—delivering messages, racking balls in poolrooms, sweeping floors—until he could get a fight. The opportunity finally came on April 26 when he knocked out Emanuel Campbell in the third round of a match sponsored by the Jockey Athletic Club. The purse was only $25, but it was a near-fortune to the young man who had hoboed into town in an empty freight car a few weeks before.

Moving on to the booming mining camps of central Nevada, Dempsey gained a small measure of fame in Goldfield by soundly thrashing a town bully, but it was work in the mines which put beans on the table since he was unable to get a paying match. Jake Goodfriend, a Tonopah saloonkeeper, was willing to take a chance on him, however, and he arranged a fight with Johnny Sudenberg, an experienced heavyweight with forty victories to his credit. Dempsey decisioned Sudenberg in ten rounds on June 13, 1915, and beat him again in Goldfield three weeks later, July 3.

The young brawler's next three fights, all victories, were staged in Utah, but he was back in Ely to meet Sudenberg again in February of 1916. Dempsey knocked him out in the second round that time and Sudenberg gave up the fight game. Two months later, April 8, 1916,

Jack Dempsey, left, at the fairgrounds in Reno at the time of the Baer-Uzcudun Fight, July 4, 1931. From left, Dempsey, Reno Mayor E. E. Roberts, James McKay, a backer of the fight, Reno Police Chief John M. Kirkley and Washoe County Sheriff Russell Trathen. (Nevada Historical Society.)

Dempsey defeated Joe Bond in the same arena and was back again in October to take the measure of Terry Keller. His last Nevada fight before he became Heavyweight Champion was a one-round knock-out of Jack Moran in Reno, on September 14, 1918.

Dempsey was an earnest, likeable sort—a man who made fast friends where he went and who never forgot those who had helped him when times were hard. In 1937, long after the glory years were over, Dempsey interceded with the U.S. Postmaster General to enable the railroad into Goldfield to keep a valuable government mail contract, the only piece of business which was keeping the line running. He also tried to help another friend, Herman "Hank" Greenspun, publisher of the Las Vegas Sun, who had gotten himself into a peck of trouble in 1949 for smuggling weapons to Israel. His efforts in Washington D.C. were unavailing, but he made the effort. It was Dempsey's way.

Among the most valuable friends that Dempsey made in Central Nevada were two men who were to later figure in another chapter in his life, Bill Graham and Jim McKay. Graham and McKay later became important figures in Reno's criminal underworld in the 'Twenties and the 'Thirties and were the owners of the Bank Club at the time of the legalization of gambling in 1931. Dempsey had been a heavy financial loser in the Stock Market Crash of 1929, and he showed up in Reno in April of 1931 with an eye to recouping his fortunes. Shortly after he arrived, he became the front man for the construction of a new casino at Reno's fairgrounds and a revamped race track. He also joined Graham and McKay in the promotion of one of Nevada's most memorable prize fights, a twenty-rounder between Max Baer and Paolino Uzcudun on July 4, 1931.

At the time of his visit to Reno in 1931, Dempsey was considering a comeback try and he entered upon his first fight in this ill-fated quest at the Reno fairgrounds arena on August 19, 1931. Following a three-week tour of the Pacific Northwest in which he met nineteen opponents, he returned to Reno to highlight a Labor Day card on September 7. He met and defeated three men that day: Eddie Burns, Sam Baker and Red Tingley. His comeback ended on February 18, 1932, when he was badly mauled in a Chicago exhibition by King Levinsky, but he was back in Nevada that summer to promote a second fight in Reno, Levinsky vs. Max Baer.

Dempsey also had mining interests in Nevada and was associated with both financier George Wingfield and mining entrepreneur Nobel Getchell in several ventures. Nevada Governor Fred Balzar was a good friend and a hunting and fishing companion, but Dempsey is best remembered in central Nevada. In May of 1950, on the occasion of Tonopah's sesquicentennial, he was the guest of honor at a dinner at the Mizpah Hotel. He renewed old acquaintances that evening and took a retrospective look of his early years in Nevada.

Jack Dempsey is gone, but he is remembered—and will be to the end of time. Tonopah's annual boxing tournament has been named in his honor, and young fighters flock to town each year in hopes of someday reaching the heights attained by Dempsey in the fistic world. There are no monuments or statues to Jack Dempsey, but the inspiration of his example is tribute enough for any man.

Tex Rickard: Monarch of the Ring

OF ALL THE men who raised a stake and got a start in Nevada, none was quite the equal of George Lewis "Tex" Rickard. A teenage cowboy from Texas who moved on to fame and fortune as a gambler in Alaska during the Klondike Gold Rush of the 1890s, Rickard is best remembered today as America's foremost boxing promoter, an avocation he first took up in Nevada.

Coming to the state in 1904, Rickard opened the Northern Saloon in Goldfield, and soon became the community's leading citizen. He owned mines in Bovard and Pioneer, and developed copper properties in White Pine County. In September of 1906, he promoted the famed lightweight championship fight between Joe Gans and Oscar "Battling" Nelson, one of the most memorable fistic events in history. Started as a promotional stunt for Goldfield and its mines, the fight put Rickard himself into the national limelight, a position he was to maintain for the next quarter of a century. In January of 1909, Rickard promoted a featherweight match between the reigning champion, Abe Attell, and Freddie Weeks, a Tonopah man who claimed the championship in that class in Colorado, Montana and Nevada. Rickard's crowning achievement in Nevada was the promotion of the historic "Fight of the Century" between Jack Johnson and Jim Jeffries in Reno on July 4, 1910.

Rickard left the United States for Paraguay in 1912, spending three years running a cattle ranch in the Gran Chaco, and returned to this country in 1915 to reenter the fight game. It began with the promotion of Jess Willard's first defense of the heavyweight crown he had recently won from Jack Johnson in Havana, Cuba. Rickard promoted several of Willard's fights and soon became the nation's best-known fight figure, but it was not until he signed his man for a match with an up-and-coming brawler from the West, Jack Dempsey, that he achieved an enduring place in ring history. It was with Dempsey that Rickard staged the greatest boxing spectaculars and

From left, Tex Rickard, George Siller and Joe Gans, principals in the famed Gans-Nelson Fight in Goldfield, September, 1906. (Nevada Historical Society.)

racked up the most awe inspiring attendance figures and gate receipts in the history of the game.

A tall, engaging man, Rickard adopted a snap-brim fedora hat and a gold-headed Malacca cane as his trademarks. Although he dressed like a dandy, he had an aura of the West about him—something of the wide-open spaces, saddles and rustlers, sheriffs, six-guns, dance halls and saloons. Gazing in awe as the crowds gathered for one of his fight promotions, he was often heard to drawl in wonder, "I never seed anything like it." A born politician and a compromiser, Rickard was not above paying off and making secret deals to obtain a promoter's license, a contract or a stadium. He was not necessarily dishonest in his easygoing approach to ethics, but knew how to balance business risks with gambler's odds and was a good judge of men.

His experience in running gambling houses in Alaska and Nevada taught him all he needed to know about the "money-fever" which infected most men. In Goldfield, he dumped the full amount of the purse for the Gans-Nelson fight, $32,000 in $10 and $20 gold pieces, into the window of the Northern to advertise the fight. He pulled a similar stunt to get Jack Johnson to sign with him in 1910. He bought Johnson's wife a new fur coat and advanced the black champion $2,500 in $100 bills for a tip on the amount of the highest bid. Johnson suggested $101,000 and Rickard got the fight. When Rickard guaranteed Dempsey and Georges Carpentier the unheard-of sum of $1,000,000 for a championship fight in July of 1921, everyone thought he was crazy. Yet the mere fact that this much money had been put up drew so many fans that they produced the largest crowd in history up to that time: 80,183 souls, and $1,789,238 in box office receipts. Bigness made for bigness, Rickard reasoned; and the fight in which Gene Tunney relieved Dempsey of the heavyweight title in 1926 drew 120,757 spectators who paid $1,895,757 to see it. The second Dempsey-Tunney fight drew only 104,933 spectators, but the gate was a record $2,658,660.

Another element in Rickard's success was his knack for making the public see one fighter as the "good guy" and the other as the "bad." In the case of the Gans-Nelson fight, Gans was suspected of having thrown fights before or winning in a certain round to help certain betters, and there was a feeling around Nevada that he would do it again if the money were right. This turned out to have been speculation only, but the Johnson-Jeffries fight was another "good guy–bad guy" contest in the view of fans and sportswriters. Johnson, the first black champion in his class, had won the title in Australia in 1908 when local police broke up the match. His subsequent flaunting of contemporary racial expectations, his fondness for white women, fancy clothes and fine automobiles and his lippy way of standing up to his critics alienated white America. Jim Jeffries, brought out of retirement as "The Great White Hope," was the "good guy" in the fight. The racial controversy thus focused international attention on the match and made it a huge promotional success.

Jess Willard's victory over Jack Johnson in 1915 was clouded by a rumor that the black champion had thrown the fight in exchange for a promise by the U.S. Justice Department to drop a morals conviction which had forced him into exile. Jack Dempsey's match with Willard in 1919 was also controversial since many Americans considered Dempsey a "slacker" and a draft-dodger during the recent war. Those who came to see Willard beat Dempsey to a pulp were to be disappointed, however. The fight went only three rounds, and Willard suffered as sound a defeat as any champion in the history of the ring.

Rickard also had a special relationship with the press. He felt that he had a right to publicity puffs and praise; and when a reporter would hint that one of his promotions might turn out to be a stinker, he would often say plaintively in his soft Texas drawl, "You fellows ought'n to be knocking. You ought to be boosting my shows. What you fellows always knocking for? Knocking don't help no one." The truth was that Rickard had every sportswriter on the hook with his Midas touch, the expanding universe of his promotions and the drama of his life. Any scribe who did not keep up with him would soon be losing his readers left and right and his job as well.

Boxing fans today have no conception of the atmosphere of turn of the century prize fighting—the low dives where the fights took place, the stench of unwashed bodies, the danger of toughs and knuckleduster artists, pickpockets, drunks and other assorted types who lived on the fringe of the fight world. It was literally worth your life to attend a fight, and you never got the seat your ticket called for. In addition, it was simply no place to take a lady. Rickard changed all that. The tickets to his fights at Madison Square Garden bore portal, aisle, section and seat numbers, and he hired special police for protection and to keep order. It became as safe for a woman and her escort to attend a Rickard fight as it was to go to the theatre.

Rickard elevated boxing from the wretched, smoke-filled arenas into the realm of glittering, royal extravaganzas perfumed by the smell of money. Prior to Rickard's time, only tennis and polo had touched the pockets and fancy of the wealthy, but he was soon to change all that. He made his play for New York's upper crust in 1920 by promoting a charity boxing match in the Garden for Miss Anne Morgan, the sister of J. P. Morgan, who was raising funds for the American Committee for Devastated France. He pitted Benny Leonard against Richie Mitchell for the lightweight championship. For the first time, the snobs packed the arena and were treated to one of the most thrilling brawls in lightweight history. They have never stopped coming.

Deep down, Rickard himself was a snob and a social climber. He did not care to break into the ranks of society, but he wanted to be patronized by those who thought of themselves as being part of the "better element." It made him feel good, he who had never had any educational or social advantages, to see the cream of New York's social strata come to him to buy tickets for his promotions.

Rickard took out a lease on Madison Square Garden in 1920 and began to promote rising unknowns in the boxing world, six day bicycle races, rodeos and carnivals. In 1924, the Democratic National Convention was held in the Garden, and Rickard began putting together the financing to construct a new Garden on Eighth Avenue. He was able to touch his wealthy friends for financial assistance, and he came out every day during the construction to watch over the work like a child with a new puppy.

Although the new Garden was an immediate success, problems with the New York Boxing Commission and Tammany Hall politicians forced him to stage his major promotions elsewhere. The match between Dempsey and Carpentier was held at Boyle's Thirty Acres in Jersey City, New Jersey, and the famous Dempsey–Luis Firpo contest was staged at the Polo Grounds. The two Dempsey-Tunney fights were put on in Philadelphia and Chicago.

In spite of his fame, or perhaps because of it, Rickard had his share

of legal difficulties and personal tragedies. He was constantly involved in litigation with other promoters and financiers who resented the intrusion of the ex-faro dealer into their territory. He was
also plagued with prosecutions over the inter-state shipment of fight
films. Other suits came about over a Texas oil scheme he engineered
in 1924, and a venture into oil leases in Guatemala. At one point, he
went through a harrowing courtroom ordeal involving morals
charges, but was acquitted. Rickard's first wife had died in child-
birth in Texas, and a brief second marriage to an Alaskan saloon
singer ended in divorce. A beloved adopted daughter died in Ely in
1907; and Edith Mae, his third wife, passed away in October of 1925,
shortly before the new Madison Square Garden opened. In 1926, he
married Maxine Hodges, an actress. Thirty years younger than Rickard, she not only presented him with a daughter in 1927, but got him
to ease up and relax. He bought a yacht, took up golf and purchased a
home on one of the lagoons near Miami, Florida. He had been forced
out of the management of the Garden by that time, but was still
promoting fights and was captivated by the notion of establishing an
American Monte Carlo in Miami, complete with a luxurious gambling casino, a hotel, a dog and horse track and an arena.

The man whose life was one long, uninterrupted drama died
unspectacularly of a gangrenous appendix on January 6, 1929. His
body was brought to New York City to lie in state in a $15,000
bronze casket in the center of the arena which he had built. Jack
Dempsey wept openly at the sight of his old friend, as did those
whom Rickard had touched in the course of his long life—the aged
and broken-faced boxers, the hardened rival promoters, the venal
politicians, the kids now grown to adulthood who remembered the
dimes that Rickard would pass out in front of the Garden. One
newsman who had covered Rickard for years was moved by the
thousands of mourners who shuffled endlessly past the body. "I
could never quite determine whether they came because Rickard's
last show was free," he later wrote, "because they were curious, or
because they had a genuine affection for this stranger from the
West."

In any case, the mourners were the rear-guard of a vanished era of
which Tex Rickard was the foremost symbol. The Great Crash of
1929 was only nine months away, and thereafter the good old days

got old very quickly. It is difficult to separate Tex Rickard from his times since the 'Twenties was a period which was ripe for the kind of extravaganzas he staged. If he had come along ten years later, a sobered-up America might have been unwilling or unable to shell out $25 to $50 for seats.

Ironically, Rickard's death contributed to that of another who was also a link with a bygone era, Wyatt Earp. Although he had been ill for some time in Los Angeles, Earp left his bed the day before Rickard died to send a telegram to his old friend. The exertion caused him to have a relapse and he died eight days later, January 13, 1929.

In 1952, an athletic stadium in Rickard's home town of Henrietta, Texas, was named in his honor; but the only remembrances of his Nevada years are two historical markers, one in Goldfield and a second in Reno. The latter, erected at the site of the Johnson-Jeffries Fight, was dedicated on July 4, 1979. Among those present that day was Maxine Texas Rickard Halprin, his daughter, and Bert Lundy, a man who had known Rickard in Goldfield and who had attended the 1910 fight. The great promoter would have been properly appreciative of the words spoken of him at the dedication, but he would have reveled in the fact that he was still remembered by those who follow the fight game a half-century after his death. It is as big a monument as any man could hope to have.

The Fight of the Century

ON JULY 4, 1910, the eyes and ears of much of the entire civilized world were focused on Reno, a raucous railroad town which was the host city for the "Fight of the Century," a heavyweight boxing match between the reigning champion of the world, John Arthur "Jack" Johnson, and James J. "Jim" Jeffries, a former champion, who had been pressured into making a comeback.

Johnson, the first black champion of the heavyweight division, had held the title since his defeat of Tommy Burns in Australia in 1908; and white America was searching for a "Great White Hope" to take it away from him. Johnson's "uppity" attitude and his fondness for fine clothes, fast cars and white women galled white America's very soul. The contest thus became a symbol of the nation's racial divisions rather than just another ballyhooed boxing match between two men.

Jeffries held the title from 1899 to 1905 and had never lost a match in his entire career. Although he had never even been knocked off his feet, he let himself go after his retirement and never was able to get in shape for a comeback. As he later admitted, it was a fight he never wanted and never felt prepared for.

Because San Francisco rather than Reno was the site originally selected by promoter Tex Rickard, both fighters set up training camps in California, Jeffries near Ben Lomand and Johnson in San Francisco. Both men went into serious training in April of 1910, but publicity surrounding the fight raised the dander of those who opposed prize fighting. A national letter-writing campaign to pressure Governor James Gillett into stopping the fight got underway, and on June 15 he ordered his Attorney General to take that move. California's laws allowed only "sparring matches," but the laws had never been tested in the courts. The real pressure on the governor came from the U.S. Congress which was considering various sites for the upcoming Panama-Pacific International Exposition to take place in 1915 in celebration of the completion of the Panama Canal. Gillett

176

Kid Cotten, Billy Jordan, and Jack Johnson, Reno, July 4, 1910. (Nevada Historical Society.)

was "subtly" informed that Congress could never consider a city so "immoral" as to permit a prize fight.

Fight fans from all over America, outraged at this turn of events, threatened to turn their tickets back and cancel their transportation arrangements. Promoter Rickard chose to seek another site immediately rather than take the matter to court. As word of the governor's action spread across the country, Rickard was deluged with offers from several dozen cities; but he had already decided to bring the fight to Nevada, a state whose prize fight laws were as liberal as any in the nation. In addition, Rickard's ties to the Silver State were strong and deep, and he had many friends and former business associates here. Rickard had already promoted the famous Gans-Nelson light heavyweight championship contest held in Goldfield in September of 1906.

Although the offers of financial support and other inducements continued to come in, Rickard decided upon Reno as the site and sent his advance men over the Sierra within hours of receiving word of Governor Gillett's decision. A meeting was held with a hastily organized group of Reno businessmen that night and the decision was made. The businessmen, organized as the Reno Athletic Association, agreed to put up a 20,000 seat arena, pay the $1,000 license fee for the fight and guarantee a $250,000 return at the gate.

Within hours of the announcement that Reno was selected, San Francisco speculators reserved all the rooms at Reno's major hotels—the Riverside, the Golden and the Overland—and contacts were made for training sites. Jeffries's manager chose Moana Hot Springs just south of Reno, but Johnson's managers had a problem finding a place for their man. Jack Vera offered his Del Monte Resort property, but Johnson's manager preferred a less populated area more suited to roadwork. Lawton's Springs west of Reno was initially chosen, but the manager had a "no Negro" policy, and Rick's Resort on the road to Verdi was selected.

Reno was meanwhile being engulfed by the first of some 30,000 fight fans descending on the little town whose population was less than 11,000 at that time. Restaurant operators laid in a stock of food and drink to take care of them, and several enterprising Renoites got together and ordered several thousand cots from California which were to be placed in hallways and alleys and rented out at $10 a night. Private homes were also opened up, as were abandoned buildings all over town including the former Nevada-California-Oregon Railroad Depot, vacant on Plaza Street. Men by the hundreds still slept in the parks and the alleys. Accommodations in nearby Sparks were also filled to capacity, and the Southern Pacific Railroad began putting in extra sidetracks outside of town to handle the dozens of Pullman Cars which would be bringing in fight fans from all over the country.

Reno's clergymen were somewhat less than pleased with their city's good fortune, however, and protested vehemently. "Repugnant to all moral sensibilities," some charged, "Godless wallowers in the muck before the Temple of Mamon," others wailed; but the preparations for the fight went forward, and the contest soon became something of a national fixation as famous figures of the boxing world came to town and renowned sports writers showed up to cover it for those not fortunate enough to be on the scene.

As the day of the fight neared, Johnson and Jeffries took up residence at their respective camps and resumed the training regimens so rudely interrupted by the forced move to Reno. Jeffries's camp at Moana could be easily reached by streetcar and the famous ex-champion drew large crowds to the resort, but Jeffries himself seemed uninterested in public adoration and indifferent to the fans. He appeared to resent their presence and would often call off a training session on the spur of the moment and leave on a fishing trip up the Truckee River. Johnson's camp at Rick's Resort, on the other hand, could be reached only by auto, but those who took the trouble to come out were amply rewarded. Joking and talking with the fans as he worked out, he would often invite them in to have a few drinks, play a little poker and listen to the jazz band that he had installed. Johnson was also open and friendly to newsmen, leading to the feeling among many writers that he would have been the .favorite had it not been for his color.

An arena site just east of town was selected, and work on the 20,000 seat structure got underway on June 22. Sheriff Ferrell made arrangements to bring in a contingent of State Police from Carson City to assist him in keeping order in Reno and to be on hand in case race riots broke out during or after the fight. Although Governor Denver Dickerson was in Oregon until June 28, he indicated by telegram that he would interpose no obstacles to the fight being held in his state. His office in Carson City was deluged with letters and telegrams from those who opposed the holding of the fight, but Senator George D. Pyne of Esmeralda County, the President Pro Tempore of the State Senate who was in charge during the governor's absence, consigned them to the wastebasket as fast as they came in.

Among those in Reno to cover the fight were writers Jack London, Rex Beach and Western gunfighter turned sportswriter Bat Masterson. Most of the luminaries of the fight world, past and present, were also in town, as were hordes of cripples begging in the streets, fast-buck artists of every description, drifters looking for excitement and girls of "easy virtue" plying their ancient trade. Reno's "better element" had not given up and were trying to persuade Mayor Arthur M. Britt to put an end to the madness which had suddenly descended upon their town. The Women's Christian Temperance Union was up in arms, and many parents forbade their children even to read the newspapers, which were filled with nothing but fight news.

Millions of dollars were riding on the fight all over the world, and most of it was on Jeffries to make a successful comeback. In Reno, the downtown betting parlors had the ex-champion at 10 to 7 to win, but the odds merely reflected the hopes of the white majority rather than the relative merits and real chances of the two fighters. Those who were able to judge fighters put their money on the black champion.

The day of the fight spectators began to arrive at 11:00 A.M., but those from out of town remained in their Pullman Cars just behind the arena until just before fight time, 3:00 P.M. The special closed off section for women was filled by noon, and all was in readiness for the momentous contest. Following the introduction of other fighters, the two principals came out, the crowd almost silent as Johnson entered the ring, but applauding and ecstatic when Jeffries appeared.

The fight itself seemed almost anticlimactical, Johnson handling Jeffries with ease and talking to him all the while. "Still think I'm yellow, Mr. Jim?" he said as he landed a series of punches. "Go ahead, take a swing, Mr. Jim, you might get lucky." Fight fans quickly picked up on the fact that Jeffries was not the man he had once been. But for Johnson's desire to put on a show, the black champion could have ended it as early as the third round. The fight went fifteen rounds, Johnson finally battering Jeffries to the canvas three times in succession that last round before cries of "Stop it, stop it" and "Don't let the old man be knocked out" came from all sides. Jeffries's own seconds then called a halt, and referee Rickard raised Johnson's arm in victory.

The crowd was momentarily stunned at the defeat of Jeffries. They broke into a cheer as Jeffries got to his feet and was helped out of the arena, but Johnson was congratulated only by his trainers and his white wife, Etta, who had been at ringside. Rabid fans were meanwhile cutting up the ropes and the canvas as souvenirs, and the boxed up ticket stubs were being hauled away to be sold for the same purpose later.

Memories of the great fight have faded over the years and even the location has been in doubt, but a group of dedicated local historians have recently been able to place it at the block between Toano and Montello Streets on the south side of what is today east Fourth Street. A historical marker now reminds visitors of the significance of the great contest.

Index

Italic page numbers denote illustrations